THE
POWER
WITHIN

The FIVE DISCIPLINES
of PERSONAL EFFECTIVENESS

Allen Johnson

Executive
Excellence
Publishing

For permissions requests, contact the publisher at:
Executive Excellence Publishing
1344 East 1120 South
Provo, UT 84606
phone: 1-801-375-4060
toll free: 1-800-304-9782
fax: 1-801-377-5960
www.eep.com

For Executive Excellence books, magazines and other products, contact Executive Excellence directly. Call 1-800-304-9782, fax 1-801-377-5960, or visit our Web site at www.eep.com.

Printed in the United States

10 9 8 7 6 5 4 3 2 100

Cover design by Jim Easley

Printed by Publishers Press

Library of Congress Cataloging-in-Publication Data

Johnson, Allen, 1946-
   The power within : the five disciplines of personal effectiveness / Allen Johnson.
   p. cm.
Includes bibliographic references and index.
   ISNB 1-890009-82-2 (hard : alk. paper)
   1. Conduct of life. 2. Discipline. 3. Self-management (Psychology) I. Title.
   BJ1595 .J44 2000
   158.1--dc21
                                                    00-008345

To my parents,
Helen and Thurston,
who taught me right from wrong
and the discipline to choose wisely.

Advance Praise for *The Power Within*

"Anyone who reads *The Power Within* will be inspired. I would read 10 pages at a time and find them talking back to me throughout the day. Thoughts would jump out, forcing me to evaluate my motives and actions. God has inspired Allen to share a message of mercy, grace, and kindness. Great reading!"

—Ann Kiemel Anderson
Author of *Seduced by Success*

"Allen Johnson walks his talk! *The Power Within* is loaded with powerful personal examples that show how the five disciplines can change your life."

—Al Seibert, Ph.D.
Author of *The Survivor Personality*

"These days loyalty to a noble cause seems to be a vanishing commodity Allen Johnson persuasively teaches that true commitment springs from an inner choice. Although his technique is delightfully varied—cajoling, prodding, reasoning—his message is straightforward: build commitment by building character."

—Robert Cialdini
Author of *Influence: Science and Practice*

"Professional athletes understand the importance of personal discipline, but Allen Johnson takes my game to a whole new level. I don't know anyone who more clearly understands the four links of discipline: body, heart, mind, and soul. When it comes to discipline, Johnson is tough to beat; if he were a football player, he'd be a nose guard."

—Kimo von Oelhoffen, NFL nose guard
Pittsburgh Steelers

"We are not called to be successful in one aspect of our lives. We are called to be successful in *all* aspects of our lives. In his winning way, Allen Johnson demonstrates how harnessing *The Power Within* leads to personal fulfillment, and professional success."

—Bill Halamandaris
Author of *Be the Light*

"Allen Johnson, with *The Power Within*, conveys powerful, important, practical messages. He does so with an unforgettable flair for telling tales—sharing the wisdom of others as well as his own. This is not a book of simple platitudes, rather one of enduring insight. Allen is a man who walks his talk and lives as an example of the disciplines he shares."

—Mahan Khalsa
Author of *Let's Get Real or Let's Not Play*
Vice President, Franklin Covey, Sales Performance Group

"In a world where it is easy to feel misaligned, Allen Johnson offers true liberation. Half philosopher, half storyteller and all business, Johnson returns meaning and truth to the workplace and the home front. This is a book to be read again and again."

—Marta Tracy, Creative Executive,
Senior Vice President, Style, E! Networks

"Peak performance is not a fluke; it doesn't happen by accident. It happens through discipline. Allen Johnson's wonderful book shows the way. Through real-life examples and crystal clear reason, he reveals the fiber of real champions."

—Dr. Edwin J. Nolan,
Director of Training and Development, Eckerd Corporation

"This book had an immediate and positive influence on my dealings with coworkers and family. *The Power Within* is an owner's manual for human beings."

—John Sheehan, Manager, Regulatory Training
Bristol-Myers Squibb Company

"*The Power Within* is a must read: it is visionary, optimistic, and practical. It has all the sense of the ages, with powerful messages for managers, teachers, leaders, and parents."
—Richard L. Anderson, President and CEO
Edge Learning Institute

"Past experiences and vivid memories come back at me with a vengeance with each reading of *The Power Within*. This guidebook is a reminder of the simple truth . . . I can do better!"
—Tom Nickel, Director, Training and Development
ARINC

"In a world of countless motivational books, here is a work of universal and timeless truths—something to be read again and again and shared with others. Allen Johnson gives us the blueprint for putting love back in our lives. He is peerless at teaching that leadership is the art of loving."
—Chris Belland, CEO
Historic Tours of America

"*The Power Within* is a book for our times. Allen Johnson gives us a good dose of what we need: the discipline to take charge of our lives once and for all. If this book doesn't motivate you, nothing will."
—Brad Fisher, Managing Director of Investments
US Bancorp Piper Jaffray

"Allen Johnson is a master storyteller who writes with a purity of heart that is so compelling that the reader is swept up by his teachings. *The Power Within* is vital nourishment for the heart and soul of any leader!"
—Cliff Reyle, Director of Human Resources
Youth Villages

"This book is a must for anyone who is serious about personal leadership. The ideas are so simple, yet so compelling, that it has the power to transform lives for good. I know first hand; Allen has had a powerful influence on our leadership team."
—Jerry Forte, Manager, Institutional Operations
Johnson Controls Northern New Mexico

"*The Power Within* is required reading for my managers. It is a book that spells out the secret of leadership from the inside-out. What is more, Johnson's life is living proof that a person can be fully actualized."
—Arnold Whipple, CEO
Informatics Corporation

"I love this book. I'm giving a copy to everyone I care about. Its depth of character stirs the heart and ignites the imagination. I am more disciplined, more joyful after having read Allen's book."
—Mark Gehlen, President
UniWest

"Picture yourself at the end of a long, but satisfying day. The image reflected back from the mirror is one of competence without arrogance, confidence without selfishness, satisfaction without complacency, spirituality without close-mindedness and, above all, a pervasive joy in living. In *The Power Within*, Allen Johnson shows how each of us can make this reflection a reality."
—Carter Johnson, President
Buying Time Seminars

"This book reads like a novel, yet packs a powerful, life-sustaining message. *The Power Within* demonstrates that you don't have to be a war hero to live a life of nobility and revolution. It's a book that has the power to turn sheep into lions. A terrific read!"
—Jerry D. Abrams, President
Jerry D. Abrams Company, Inc.

"I've never met another teacher or mentor who so completely exemplifies the principles presented in this book. He is a testament to the power within. But he also demonstrates with authority that what he has is also ours for the asking. All of us can live lives of absolute passion."

—Steve McPhee, President
IMC Consulting Inc.

"Allen Johnson is a masterful storyteller! His book, *The Power Within*, provides moving and uplifting stories that illustrate the five disciplines that define a victorious life. For those who are serious about creating a meaningful and rich journey, you will reach for *The Power Within* again and again."

—Terry Barber, Director of Professional Development
The Association of Washington School Principals

"What a refreshing read! *The Power Within* is the "jumper cables" for personal renewal. Allen Johnson's real life examples propel his belief that we all have a power within—if we choose to recognize it. This book has caused me to examine the quality of my own discipline and the relationships I have with others."

—Marcel Loh, President and CEO
Kadlec Medical Center

"*The Power Within* is a book from the mind and heart, and also from the spirit. Allen Johnson masterfully demonstrates how our spirituality is manifested in the ordinary interactions we have with others each day. His words heal the soul."

—Rev. Charles S. Vavonese,
Assistant Superintendent for Advancement
Catholic Schools Diocese of Syracuse

Acknowledgments

The power within—the disciplines of love, responsibility, vision, commitment, and service—is a birthright. However, that power may be either fanned or extinguished by parents, siblings, friends, and colleagues. Throughout my life, I have been blessed by scores of people who have encouraged my intellectual and spiritual development—people who have, by their example, borne witness to the dynamic power within. I hesitate to list these people, for I am sure to omit some names inadvertently—and for that I apologize. I have listed only the most persuasive models and loyal champions:

- My wife Nita, for her unconditional love.
- My mother and father, for their undying faith.
- My brother and his family, for undaunted courage.
- The Men's Group—Jim Bauer, Larry Birckhead, Jamie Cox, Mark Gladstone, Bill Hillar, Rick Martinez, Paul Patterson, Jim Todd, George Umbright, and Dee Willis—for their commitment to truth and understanding.
- My dearest friends, colleagues, and extended family, whose lives—past and present—provide abundant proof that, unharnessed, the power within is a joyful and magnetic force: Mike Alamia; Terry and Pat Barber; Clara Berger; Jill Blaylock; Les Brown; Joe Calhoon; Judy Clem; Jack Cloud; Dave Conley; Jim Devine; Ernie and Ruth DeWater; Carol Dice; Jack and Deanna Doying; Debi Eng; Bob and Helen

9

Estep; Paula Farnsworth; Doug Gross; Mindy Halladay; Harvey and Ida Hart; Richard and Susan Harrington; Murray Innes; Hugh and Fritzi Johnson; Jerry Johnson; Charlie and Marion Higley; Richard Johnston; my cousin, Basil Katsaros; my uncle and aunt, John and Soitera Kostikos; David and Marcile Leach; Jim and Doris Lisk; Howard and Margi Macy; Erlon and Elsie Meloy; Jim and Juanita Mullin; Earl Owens; Gene Parulis; Lois, Larry, and Ken Richwine; Jon Spangle; Lew Zirkle; and numerous colleagues at FranklinCovey Company.

- Charles Morgan and Lynn Orr, for their friendship and research assistance.
- Ed Anderson, of AndersonBell, for his kind tutelage in applying ABstat, a statistics software program.
- Countless business clients, whose professional competence is exceeded only by their depth of character: Olivia Catolico, Susie Childress, Tom Corley, Jerry Forte, Jeffery D. Hester, Steve McPhee, Pierre Saget, Addanki Sastry, Chuck Vavonese, and Arnie Whipple.
- Authors of unparalleled insight and clarity of purpose: Peter Block, Bob Buford, Stephen R. Covey, Peter F. Drucker, Wayne Dyer, William Glasser, Robert K. Greenleaf, Abraham Maslow, M. Scott Peck, and Carl Rogers.

I also add one disclaimer: Many of the names and details of people mentioned in the book have been changed to protect their privacy.

Contents

Preface

My name is Allen Johnson. I am a psychologist—at least that's my official title. Unofficially, I have been called a *headpeeper*, *bug doctor*, and a *shrink*, the latter being ironic because, when it comes right down to it, I'm really an *expander*. I believe in our capacity to create a world that is stronger, richer, and infinitely more joyful.

This book is about that creative capacity—the phenomenon I call *The Power Within*. For 30 years, I have been in the business of helping people to become more effective in their personal and professional lives. In that time, I have discovered that some people are equipped with the ability to transcend the challenges of the day. Their lives are abundant and fulfilling, bursting with joy and excitement. They encounter each new day with enthusiasm, with a vitality that is so exuberant it spills over on others, leaving unsuspecting naysayers scratching their heads and saying, "Wow, what was that?"

Meanwhile, some people stand waiting, like Meryl Streep in *The Bridges of Madison County*, for a stranger to step out of the morning sun and sweep them up and off to a magic land of perfect bliss. Unfortunately for them, the hero hardly ever appears (even when he does, he lacks the power to shake them out of their doldrums), and so they stand, their eyes morosely transfixed on the horizon, simmering in the stew of their own time-honored recipe for misery.

What makes the difference between these two opposing groups of people? That question nagged me for years. This book is my answer—my attempt to uncover the vibrant qualities that transform a life from sleepwalking to victorious living.

THE BOOK'S STRUCTURE

The Power Within describes how the five disciplines of *love, responsibility, vision, commitment,* and *service* work together to generate personal, interpersonal, and organizational well-being. The five disciplines are about action, about what people do to become more purposeful, more joyful, and more at peace.

The book is divided into two parts. Part I: *The Foundation of Effectiveness,* comprised of the first four chapters, sets the stage for the book by defining and illustrating key terms and concepts. Part II: *Five Disciplines of Effectiveness* follows with an in-depth exploration of each of the five disciplines. The Epilogue, *When We Fall Short: The Path of Humility and Spirit,* comes from the heart. It includes a determination to lay aside our shortcomings and commit to the five disciplines of personal effectiveness.

My sincere hope is that you will discover *the power within* and practice the *five disciplines* to achieve what is most meaningful to you.

Part I

THE FOUNDATION OF EFFECTIVENESS

The first four chapters define and illustrate key terms and concepts used throughout the book.

Chapter 1, "The Source: Five Higher-Order Human Competencies," sets the philosophical framework for the book. The chapter explains how discipline flows from a universal human instinct or inheritance—what I call the five higher-order human competencies: insight, moral knowledge, imagination, independent will, and self-transcendence.

Chapter 2, "The Behavior: Five Disciplines of Effectiveness," introduces the five disciplines that spring from the five human competencies. The chapter includes dramatic illustrations for each discipline—with emphasis upon converting ideology into deliberate and principle-centered action.

Chapter 3, "The Means: Awakening the Five Disciplines of Effectiveness," is dedicated to the motivation of the human spirit. Because many people fail to take full advantage of their birthright—both human competencies and disciplines—I provide a strategy for arousing and revitalizing your inheritance. The consequence is the creation of a world that is larger, richer, stronger, and more autonomous.

Chapter 4, "The Results: The Legacy of Discipline," is based on the results of my original research, work that underscores the strong, positive correlation between well-being (happiness, peace, and joyful anticipation) and the five disciplines of effectiveness. The research is drawn from a sampling of over 850 adults and teenagers and explores the differences between happy teenagers and adults and their unhappy counterparts. I include several poignant personal and professional anecdotes.

Chapter 1

HE SOURCE

FIVE HIGHER-ORDER HUMAN COMPETENCIES

In the world it is easy to live after the world's opinions. And in soli-tude it is easy to live after one's own. But the great one is he, who in the midst of a crowd, can keep with a perfect sweetness the indepen-dence of solitude.

—Ralph Waldo Emerson

I only spent 20 minutes with him, but in that brief time he became one of my heroes. He was a taxi driver with Elite Transportation, and he picked me up at my home for a 6 a.m. flight to Los Angeles. He was, perhaps, 28 years old, about five feet six, and walked with a labored gate.

I am usually quiet on these trips to the airport. A day of travel-ing across country can test my patience. Security stations, canceled flights, and deep-fried chicken sandwiches are not my idea of a good time. And as for flying, I think of it as forced intimacy at 34,000 feet above sea level. So, I'm seldom in the mood for idle chitchat—with anyone. But for some reason I was impelled to start a conversation with the young man behind the wheel.

"I always use the same taxi service," I said. "I haven't seen you before; you must be new on the job."

"Nope," the man chirped. "I've been with Elite for almost four years. But I'm moving on. I'm getting a new job in a couple of weeks with Dial-A-Ride."

"Better wages?" I asked.

"Yeah, a little, but more importantly, I like the passengers. I like to help the older people—you know, folks with hip replacements and bad knees. My heart goes out to 'em."

"Oh?"

"Yeah, I've had 32 operations myself, so I know what it's like."

I looked at the driver. I noticed something not quite right about his right hand. I decided to follow his story. "Why have you had so many operations?" I asked.

"I was born with a rare disease. It's called arthrogryposis multiplex congenita."

The words tumbled out of his mouth, like he had said them a thousand times.

"I've never heard of that before," I said meekly, wondering if I was treading on tender ground.

"Not many people have heard of it. It's a one-in-a-million birth defect. There have only been two cases in the Pacific Northwest in the last 15 years—and I'm one of 'em. It's complicated, but basically my tendons didn't grow with my body."

"How is it treated?" I asked.

"Carefully. First, you've got to find a doctor who knows something about it. That's not easy, since there isn't much written about it in medical books. When you finally find the right surgeon, he goes in and snips and stretches your tendons and then prays it's enough."

I was taken by how cheerfully Don shared his medical history.

"Wow, you must have had one traumatic childhood."

"Oh, it wasn't that bad," he said. "I had a great support team. My parents were terrific; I couldn't have done it without them."

"Okay, but you had to be harassed by other kids when you were growing up? I mean, kids can be brutal."

Don chuckled. "Yeah, that was tough. But you know what I remember? The good stuff. There was a kid I grew up with, starting from day one in kindergarten. When we graduated from high school, he came up to me and apologized for making fun of me when we were in first grade. I couldn't believe it; that meant a lot to me."

I looked intently at the profile of the young man driving down the freeway. Could he truly be that forgiving? I searched his face for some hint of sarcasm; there was none. "After all that," I said, "I can see how you would empathize with people who are disabled."

"Hey, I understand the word *ouch*."

I smiled and nodded. I really liked this guy. "How are you doing now, Don? I mean physically."

"Oh, my right hand doesn't work so well." He held out his hand for my inspection. It was cupped closed—nearly a fist. "But it still does what I want it to do, so why bother." He slipped the cupped hand over the steering wheel.

"Do you plan to have it operated on?" I asked.

"No, the percentages are lousy. But that's okay. It still does the job. 'If it ain't broke, don't fix it,' I always say."

"I admire your spirit," I said. Despite my best intentions, the words seemed hollow.

"Ah, what's to admire?" he shrugged. "Life's too short to be a grouch. My life is good. I have a beautiful wife; my car and trailer are paid off; and some day I'll trade up and buy a house. Why should I complain?"

We pulled into the airport. I was feeling dwarfed by the positive energy of this young warrior. "Thanks for your story, Don." I said. "I wish you all the luck in the world. You're an inspiration. I mean it."

Don smiled and said, simply, "Thanks."

When I stepped into the airport, I was greeted with a line of travelers that stretched nearly 50 yards. My flight had been canceled, and everyone was scrambling to make alternate flight arrangements.

I smiled and said out loud, "I can handle this."

•   •   •

THE POWER WITHIN

The basic assumption of this book is that *we all have a power within*—a wisdom that lies below the surface of our conditioning and prejudices. The fact that it often remains untapped does not negate its presence.

How do I know such a power exists? I see the evidence everywhere. The childlike satisfaction of learning a new concept is the power within. The joy of making the right choice in a difficult situation is the power within, as are the thrill of taking aim on excellence, the integrity of attending to what is important, and the rightness of serving those in need. All are evidences of the power within.

It's a joyful thing, this mighty internal power. I am not talking about the flash-in-the-pan, doubled-up, belly-laugh kind of joy (although I'm a big proponent of that too), but rather, the kind of joy that is deep and peaceful—enduring joy.

In effect, the power within is the power to derive joy from our life experiences, including our most difficult trials.

When I was a young man, I became acquainted with a Quaker minister who pastored a thriving church in Seattle. His name was David Leach. Dave and his wife Marcile took me in one summer when I was attending graduate school. I will never forget that summer.

There was something immediately engaging about Dave. He was always enthusiastic, almost giddy, about an exciting new project, and all the while, deeply interested in the lives of people. He was the first person I met who could encourage and teach without being heavy-handed about it.

In those days, my immaturity surfaced in my choice of humor; all too often it was peppered with sarcasm and putdowns. One night at the dinner table, I ridiculed someone who was not known for his intelligence. "He's not very high up on the food chain," I quipped.

Later that evening, I was sitting on the backyard deck, strumming my guitar. Dave sat down beside me. "Hey, Al," he said, "I want to talk to you about something."

"Sure, Dave."

"You really make me laugh," he said. "You have such a quick wit." And then after a pause: "I wonder if that wit could be used for better purposes?"

"What do you mean?" I asked.

"Well, you're always funny, but sometimes you're funny at the expense of others—you know, the putdowns. I would bet $100 that you're capable of developing a sense of humor that is 10 times more sophisticated."

That conversation unfolded 30 years ago, and I still remember it. Dave's message was offered so calmly, so lovingly, that I could not help but see the truth of it. His influence did not stop there. Years later, when I told Dave I was undecided about pursuing a doctorate degree, his belief in me was unequivocal—his tone matter-of-fact. "You're ready," he said. "It's your time."

That was it. In that moment I decide to go for it; four years later I had my degree. Obviously, Dave's influence was enormous. But why? Why should I have been so dramatically influenced by his words? I think it was due to his *power within*: his capacity to love, his joy for service, his sense of inner peace. I found myself wanting to be like him.

This book is about the power of people like Dave.

FIVE HIGHER-ORDER HUMAN COMPETENCIES

To release the *power within*, we must begin by understanding its source.

At the base of our skull is the medulla oblongata, the most ancient part of our brain. It controls the autonomic functions of the body, most notably the fight-or-flight instinct. This portion of the brain looks very much like the brain of a tiger. I mention that because we sometimes react like tigers—growling and pouncing—when things do not go our way.

Many people rely heavily on this primitive brain. When they are under stress—when they experience some form of psychological pain—they either attack or take flight. We often refer to these defense mechanisms as hostility and depression. Ironically, these instinctive approaches are self-defeating: Although the intent is to reduce the pain, in the long run, the pain escalates. For example, if I were jilted in love (and relied entirely on my primitive brain for direction), I might respond to the pain by pulling myself out of social circulation. That isolation, however, could spiral into depression, culminating in psychosomatic symptoms, eating disorders, addictions, psychosis, and even thoughts of suicide.

The fight-or-flight instinct rarely serves us well. It makes no sense to run and hide when our checkbook doesn't balance or get angry when someone cuts us off in traffic. Yes, the impulse may still linger, but it is a primitive impulse—one that can be tamed by the *power within*.

The source of the *power within* is the higher brain located in the cerebral cortex—the gray matter. It houses the *five higher-order human competencies*: insight, moral knowledge, imagination, independent will, and self-transcendence. By employing these competencies, we transcend the chaos and turmoil that assaults our lives. We respond with a sense of human dignity. Such responses separate those who are *out of control* from those who are *in control*.

Although we all possess these competencies, we do not possess them equally. We may be more evolved in one competency than we are in another (in fact, some competencies may be virtually dormant). Our level of maturity is a measure of these competencies working within us.

The five competencies pave the way to maturity. The more evolved these competencies in us, the more mature we will behave.

Let's take a closer look at each of the five competencies.

1: Insight

Insight, the first higher-order competency, is the foundation of mental health. People who develop this competency are living with their eyes wide open. They are fully aware of themselves, other people, and their environment.

When I travel in airplanes, I am always upset when the person in front of me reclines the seat back the instant the seatbelt light is extinguished. I don't mind that he reclines the seat—it is his right—I only mind the suddenness of the act, for often the reclining seat bumps my bad left knee.

I once decided to raise the level of awareness of the passenger in front of me, after he relocated my patella.

After rehearsing the speech in my mind, I tapped the man on the shoulder. "Excuse me, sir," I said with all the kindness I could muster. "You might want to consider reclining your chair more slowly in the future. The person behind you may not be fully prepared."

"Oh, I'm sorry," he said. "I didn't know. I wasn't thinking. I'll remember next time."

I believe him on all counts.

My point is this. No one is *fully* aware, but some people are more aware than others. Those who are more evolved in insight, see things others do not see. They hear the inconsistencies in their own language; they see the nuance of a raised eyebrow; they sense the presence of the "dead body" (the unspoken secrets) that other managers gingerly step over at the executive retreat. These people are tuned in. For example, my friend, Dave, was exercising his insight when he introduced me to the fine gradients of humor.

The more insightful we are, the more engaged we are by the joy of living. My friend, Mark, is an avid fisherman. He likes to grab his favorite rod and reel and step into the backwaters of the Columbia River where the fallen trees at water's edge create an inviting home for largemouth bass. He speaks rhapsodically about the summer days, near dusk, when the air is warm and the insects skim the water's surface. He takes it all in: the golden sun dropping behind Rattlesnake Mountain, the cool water lapping against his legs, the swish of his line whispering overhead and out to that perfect spot. At that moment Mark is fully insightful, fully aware of his surroundings, and not surprisingly, fully joyful.

The competency of insight has nothing to do with morality—it is neutral on that score. It simply collects data for examination. Determining the relative virtue of that data is the responsibility of the second human competency: moral knowledge.

2: Moral Knowledge

Moral knowledge is given many names: intuition, conscience, the inner voice, the voice of God, the Holy Spirit, the divine law written on the heart. Although people have gone to war over the name, the fact remains there is a still, small voice within—call it what you like—that guides us in determining the right thing to do.

The thing that has fascinated me is how the body is calibrated to alert us when we have violated our moral knowledge. When my body hurts—when the muscles in the back of my neck tense up, when my stomach flips, when my face reddens and my sweat glands start pumping—it's a reliable indicator that I have violated my inner voice.

Once I was booked to speak in Orlando, Florida. Because I was so close to the Caribbean, I decided to take a couple of extra days and fly to the Cayman Islands for some scuba diving. I was on a tight allowance, so I stayed in a low-budget hotel with a view of a parking lot and a brown dumpster. All the classy hotels were across the street, overlooking the ocean.

The food at the hotel where I stayed had the flavor of a TV dinner. So, on the second day I decided to try a meal at the hotel across the street.

On the back verandah next to the pool, there was a long line of people serving themselves to a buffet. Fine, I thought, a buffet would give me a chance to sample a number of island dishes.

As I waited in line, it suddenly occurred to me that the buffet might be set up for a private party. I looked for a sign. There it was: a small placard at the head of the first table. PRIVATE PARTY.

I was about to turn away when I thought, "What the hell. I've been standing here for 10 or 15 minutes. Who's going to know? There must be 300 people in this group. If I'm nabbed, I'll just tell them I didn't see the sign. Besides, there's enough food here to feed a small nation for a week. And I'll save on a free meal." Even as I was telling myself all this, I could feel the tension mounting in my shoulders and lower back.

Just then, an attractive woman in a white dress spoke to me. "Excuse me."

I knew she was talking to me, even before I turned, but I played it cool. "I'm sorry, were you speaking to me?"

"Yes, I was," she said smiling. "Are you a member of Jones International?"

"No, I'm not," I said, still playing dumb. "Why do you ask?" I was trying to sound as suave as possible.

"I'm afraid this is a private party."

"Oh, my," I said. "How stupid of me." I turned with a flare and began to stride off. But before I took a single step, the woman stopped me by grabbing my forearm. "If I were you," she said, "I would stay and eat. There is plenty of food." Her eyes looked so warm and friendly, how could I refuse?

"Are you sure it would be all right? I mean, I don't want to intrude."

"Sure, it'll be fine," said the woman in white. "Just don't let that lady catch you. She controls everything."

I followed her line of sight. She was pointing at a young brunette in a light blue apron and a name button that read, "Hi, I'm Tiffany. Have a perfect Cayman day."

"I should be able to dodge her," I said, feeling the heat on my face. "By the way, what is the business of Jones International?" I asked.

"We are in telecommunications."

As I was serving myself at the buffet table, Tiffany caught my eye. I immediately turned my attention to the potato salad directly in front of me.

When I had finished serving myself, I looked for a quiet table away from Tiffany's discerning eyes. I found an open chair at a table near the pool. I smiled and nodded politely at the six other diners at the table. They all had the same expression: "I don't know who you are, but I'll smile just in case you're someone important."

I had taken two bites of potato salad when someone whispered in my ear, "I'm sorry this is a private party. You will have to leave." I didn't even look up; I knew it was Tiffany. I picked up my plate, stood up, and slithered out the exit. I found a small table in the shadows of the hotel bar and ate my dinner in less than 60 seconds. It was the worst meal of my life. My head was reeling, and my stomach was churning. If I could have flown out that night, I would have done so.

As I crossed the street to my hotel room, I promised myself that I would never return to that ocean-side hotel. I even considered disguising myself for the rest of the weekend.

My body knew right away what I was up to—trying to get something for nothing. It warned me, and I refused to listen. But the body is insistent. You can ignore the warning signs, but eventually, inevitably, you pay for it. I paid dearly. To this day, I can't look potato salad in the face without evoking the terrifying vision of Tiffany swooping down on me like a pterodactyl.

Now, I am not proud of that story; in fact, I didn't tell anyone about this incident for a couple of years. But from it I learned once again that our conscience sounds when we do something wrong. To suggest that I could not decipher the message would be unabashed self-deception.

Some might say that it wasn't conscience working on me, that I was just embarrassed about getting caught. Yes, I was embarrassed, but that embarrassment started not when I was found out, but the moment I first decided to deceive. Real embarrassment comes with the intention to violate the conscience.

I have a friend who once argued, "Moral knowledge is nothing more than my mother's tapes playing in my head. I have been programmed."

"I agree," I replied. "You have been programmed by the same Mother Tapes that are playing in the ear of every man, woman, and child on earth." Isn't it interesting that your uniquely personal mother tapes—be kind to others, share your toys, help your brother—are so similar to my own tapes. Could it be because our private recordings are downloaded from the universal Mother Tapes? And could "Mother Tapes" just be another way of saying moral knowledge?

People often like to dispute the universality and divinity of moral conscience. I am confused as to why. Why would one want to ignore or dismiss his or her sacred self? From a purely pragmatic perspective, the benefits of abiding by moral knowledge are overwhelming. Isn't peace, in all the corridors of our lives, the ultimate benefit?

Moral knowledge supplies a basis for evaluation of the virtue of our thoughts, feelings, and experiences. It does not, however, produce a picture of what to do with that evaluation. That falls within the domain of the third human competency: imagination.

3: Imagination

Imagination is the capacity to make home movies of our thoughts. It is a versatile competency—able to create film clips that are sometimes honorable, sometimes crass. It can be a cool cup of reason or a cauldron of mindlessness. Imagination has the power to picture the pyramids of Egypt, the hanging gardens of Babylon, and the frescoes of the Sistine Chapel ceiling. It also has the power to preview something mischievous, malevolent, or tragic.

One hot, summer day, Terry, a high school friend, agreed to take my brother and me to the swimming hole in the Columbia River to cool off. The last 100 yards to the swimming hole was a steep embankment. Terry stopped the car and we got out to take a look. We decided to drive down the embankment to the water's edge. Terry got behind the wheel, but my brother and I decided to sit on the front fenders of the '52 Chevy as it coasted down the slope.

Everything was fine at first. My brother and I were laughing and punching each other in the arm as the car rolled down the hill. Then Terry decided to slam on the brakes.

My brother and I went flying off the front end of the car, our arms and legs flailing to maintain balance. Luckily we both landed on our feet in an all out sprint, but, unlike my brother, I was shoeless.

Now, the Columbia Basin in Southeastern Washington is an area famous for its tack weeds—a creeping ground cover that is adorned with rock-hard thorns with quarter-inch, needle points. For my money, they are the nastiest weeds on the planet.

As luck would have it, that embankment was blanketed in tack weeds. With every step I took, a dozen tack weeds punctured the tender soles of my feet. Then I fell down. Now my legs, arms, hands, and chest were covered with thorns—many of their needles broken and lodged under my skin.

Terry felt sick about my misfortune and pleaded for forgiveness. I thought about how forgiving I wanted to be for the next hour, while the three of us meticulously unsheathed the tiny blades from my body.

That story demonstrates both the power and the danger of imagination. What we can imagine, for good or evil, we can create. The mind is able to generate countless scenarios; some are noble and worthy of exploration, but others are misguided or mean-spirited or even obscene. That is why moral knowledge is such a critical component of the five competencies. The conscience, when operating at full capacity, provides the filter for imagination, through which all ideas are evaluated and sifted.

Imagination has been the centerpiece for many of the positive thinking, self-help books of modern times. These writers suggest that all things are created twice, once in the mind and once in reality, and that the quality of mental imagery (the first creation) determines the quality of actual behavior (the second creation). For example, the writing of this book is nothing more than imagination acted upon.

Sometimes we act too quickly on our imagination—as Terry did on that misbegotten summer day—and the second creation, the action taken, falls short of reason or virtue or value. That is why we must fully utilize the next higher-order competency: independent will.

4: Independent Will

Independent will is the human capacity to act on moral knowledge. It is called *independent* because it stands courageously unaffected by dishonorable internal or external influences. For example, it is the workings of independent will when, despite our basic instinct to be sarcastic, we choose to be kind. And you can credit independent will when, over vociferous demands for revenge, we seek reconciliation.

Independent will must not be confused with *free* will. Although both terms denote the liberty to make choices, only *independent* will signifies the liberty to make *noble* choices. Nearly every day of our lives, we see or hear of people who choose to harm others. They are acting out of free will, not independent will. I offer the following story as an example of both.

In 1962, my father-in-law, John Astleford, was serving as a Quaker missionary on the plains of Guatemala. At 39 years of age, he had already lived nearly half his life in the Central American country.

One day, John was invited to speak at the Presbyterian church in Guatemala City—a four-hour journey from John's mission in Chiquimula. One hour into the trip, John stopped at the tollbooth at the entrance of the Pan American Highway. Two young men approached his Chevrolet carryall.

"Please help us," they pleaded. "Our mother is dying, and we must go to her. It is Holy Week, and all the buses are overcrowded. Please, sir, would you be kind enough to give us a ride?"

Naturally, John invited the travelers to join him. They drove for over two hours. During that time John shared his faith with the two men. Finally, having reached the travelers' destination, John pulled off to the side of the road. "This is your stop," he said.

"Just a little farther," one of the travelers said. "Down that dirt road."

John turned onto the rutted country road, thinking nothing about it—similar lanes served many of Guatemala's villages.

A few minutes later, the other man spoke. "This is good," he said. "Right here, please."

John stopped the carryall and turned to say goodbye to his new companions. He was about to say *vaya con Dios* when he turned and found himself staring into the barrel of a revolver. John watched the man squeeze down on the trigger. The first bullet entered John's right cheek, shattering his teeth and exploding the roof of his mouth. The second bullet grazed the back of his neck. Quickly, the two men shoved their victim under the dash. Incredibly, John remained conscious; he could hear them talking.

"Keep looking," one of them said frantically. "He's an American. He must have a lot of money."

Moments later the *bandidos* were gone. John slowly pulled himself up and onto the seat. He grabbed a hand towel from the glove compartment and pressed the cloth against the gaping hole on the side of his face.

Somehow, fighting to remain conscious, John managed to drive 20 kilometers to the American Hospital in Guatemala City. Two nurses, who, ironically, had graduated from the mission school in Chiquimula, were coming off duty when John careened to a stop at the emergency door. Quickly, the nurses half walked, half carried the bleeding man into the hospital.

John, still conscious, motioned for a pencil and paper. What would he write? *I have no mouth. Tell my family I love them.* No. These were the words he scrawled: "My name is John Astleford. Please tell the Presbyterian church I will not be able to fulfill my commitment."

One week later, a policeman escorted a handcuffed man into John's hospital room.

"Is this the man who shot you?" the policeman asked.

John looked at the unshaven man. His head was down; it looked like his legs would give out at any moment. The policeman lifted the prisoner's head by yanking a stock of the man's long, black hair. There was no question; he was the shooter. John was silent for a moment. Then, without warning, the prisoner began to weep.

"What is your name?" John asked.

His eyes downcast, the prisoner said, "Manuel."

"Did I offend you, Manuel?"

"No, you only talked about God."

The room fell silent. Still, Manuel could not bear to look at the man he had shot in the face.

"Manuel," John said.

Slowly, for the first time, the prisoner lifted his eyes.

"I forgive you."

Let us understand the significance of this story. When Manuel pulled the trigger, he was exercising his free will (a universal human privilege), but only his free will. In contrast, John's free will—tempered by years of incorporating all five competencies—had long before been transformed into *independent* will (the capacity to act on moral knowledge).

As an epilogue to John's story, one month after the shooting, John was scheduled to revisit a plastic surgeon who was to begin reconstructive surgery on the roof of his mouth. But there was no work to be done. Inconceivably, the gap had closed on its own. The surgeon, a man of science, was beside himself. He jumped back, ran to the door, flung it open, and screamed to his nurses. "Look at this!" he shouted. "It's a miracle! My God, it's a miracle!"

John would continue to serve the people of Guatemala for the next 26 years. Now retired, he continues to prove that his independent will is still vital; although now in his eighties, he serves as a missions adjunct translator. His life has been a testament to the power of independent will and to the spirit of the last human competency: self-transcendence.

5: Self-transcendence

Self-transcendence is the human capacity to subordinate self-interest to the welfare of others. The competency emerges from the core of the higher self and is made evident by the calling to serve, to make a contribution, to forgive, to transcend personal desires for the sake of others. This is the highest, most evolved human competency. For most it does not come early in life (for some it does not come at all). It requires a tender heart, one that has out-grown adolescent self-absorption—a quality in no way restricted to teenagers. It requires a heart like Emily's.

A friend of mine volunteers to work at a local hospice facility once a week. That in itself is an act of self-transcendence, but not nearly as compelling as the story of one of his hospice patients.

Emily was 45 years old and dying of cancer. Her case was so advanced that she could no longer walk without assistance. Because the woman was extremely overweight, it took two strong people to maneuver her out of her bed and to the bathroom.

Once a week Emily was wheeled to a small shower stall. On this occasion she sat down on a plastic stool in the shower and let the hot water cascade over her head and down her back. She thought of it as one of life's greatest pleasures.

"Are you all right?" asked Carmen, the head nurse.

Emily looked up and smiled. "Yes."

"Can I leave you alone for a moment?"

Again, "Yes."

But Emily was not all right. Within a couple of minutes she slumped over, unconscious. When she was discovered, two nurses and my friend tried to lift Emily out of the stall. But the shower was too small and Emily nearly filled the porcelain cubical to capacity. The nurses could not get their arms around her. Emily could not be budged.

They called 911. In minutes four strapping medics were on the scene. They worked for 10 minutes, stepping here, prying there, until finally, the four men, now in a full sweat, were able to slide Emily out of the stall. There she lay sprawled on the tile, a flannel sheet draped over her body, her head in Carmen's lap. Emily's bladder emptied itself.

It was at that moment that Emily regained consciousness. She slowly surveyed the room: the seven men and women looking down at her limp body in a pool of her own urine. She looked into the worried eyes of the woman who held her head. In that instant, she fully understood what had happened. Again, her eyes turned to Carmen; the nurse was pale, so overcome with concern.

Emily raised her hand and stroked the nurse's hair: "Don't worry, Carmen" she said. "I'm okay. I just blacked out." And then, still cradled in the nurse's arms, Emily smiled and asked this question: "Carmen, are you all right?"

That is self-transcendence. That kind of other-centeredness—to place the welfare of others above one's own ego—does not come without persistent effort. It requires a full realization of the four preceding higher-order competencies—insight, moral knowledge, imagination, and independent will—and a spiritual orientation.

To activate all five higher-order competencies is to tap the very essence of our soul. There are those who would say we are only temporal beings. I adamantly disagree. Our spirituality is made evident each time we draw on the five competencies—and is ultimately manifested through the procreation of peace. When we create peace for ourselves, and make peace with others, we have tapped our spiritual selves.

The business card of Mother Teresa had these four lines imprinted on the reverse side.

The fruit of silence is prayer.
The fruit of prayer is love.
The fruit of love is service.
The fruit of service is peace.

To a great extent the five competencies are captured in those words. Do not insight and moral knowledge emanate from prayer? Do not imagination and the deliberate action of independent will grow out of love? And is not self-transcendence expressed through service and manifested in peace?

But there is a problem. The five competencies cannot, by themselves, guarantee spiritual maturation, because—and this is very important to understand—*the five competencies are only raw faculties. They remain dormant (or misused) until they are transformed into action through the five disciplines of personal effectiveness.* You can think of the five competencies as inactive ingredients that require the catalyst of discipline to come alive.

Chapter 2

HE BEHAVIOR

FIVE DISCIPLINES OF EFFECTIVENESS

Preach the gospel at all times; if necessary, use words.
—St. Francis of Assisi

Many of us hate to talk about discipline. When I told a friend that I was writing on the subject, he drew out an imaginary foil and started fencing. "Begone you heartless blackguard," he said, gleefully running me through. And why shouldn't he? We naturally associate *discipline* with starvation diets and Marine Corps workouts. Relax. That is not the kind of discipline I am talking about. That old-fashioned notion of discipline—let's call it *compliance*, to make a distinction—is about adherence to superficial, if not arbitrary, rules. The kind of discipline I am speaking about—exceedingly richer and more joyful—is about adherence to timeless principles of effectiveness.

Still, discipline is not easy. The word *discipline* comes from the Latin *disciplina*, meaning pupil. The disciplined person is, indeed, a pupil, moving from the *natural* state of ignorance and disorder to the *unnatural* state of understanding and control. We naturally follow the course of least resistance. We tend to avoid confrontation, shun physical exercise, even evade self-examination. I am always bemused by clients who, after one session, are miraculously cured. They call minutes before the second session to announce that all is well: their lives are, once again, in perfect order. That is what they say. Truth be known, they were simply unwilling to pay the price of making hard changes, unwilling to give up the course of least resistance—for, when it comes right down to it, in the dark labyrinth of depression, living with misery seems less daunting than taking responsibility.

Laziness is the natural state of many human beings, and, yet, people do grow—physically, intellectually, socially, spiritually. Every college graduation, every apprenticeship served, every challenging project taken on and completed, every relationship healed is evidence of our capacity to overcome our affinity for laziness. How does that happen? Through the unnatural acts of the five disciplines of effectiveness.

In this chapter, we will examine the five disciplines, but first, let's be clear about our definition of discipline. *Discipline is the conversion of the five higher-order competencies into principle-centered behaviors. In turn, principles are timeless, natural laws that transcend all political and social boundaries* (love, forgiveness, and respect are examples).

THE FIVE DISCIPLINES OF EFFECTIVENESS

The five disciplines of effectiveness are love, responsibility, vision, commitment, and service. The five competencies serve all five disciplines, however each discipline has its own "mother" competency—a competency that is particularly nurturing of the specific discipline. For example, the discipline of *love* is nurtured by the competency of *insight:* "to know me is to love me." Similarly, responsible behavior emanates from moral knowledge; a noble vision is served by imagination; commitment to truth flows from the honor of independent will; and service grows out of the competency of self-transcendence.

The five disciplines	The five associated competencies
Love	Insight
Responsibility	Moral knowledge
Vision	Imagination
Commitment	Independent will
Service	Self-transcendence

Think of the relationship in this way: the five competencies are the driving force of the five disciplines. The five competencies are natural, latent capacities—a *potential* way of being; the five disciplines are behaviors, the five competencies acted upon—a mode of conduct. Now, let's discuss each of the five disciplines.

1. The Discipline of Love:
From Ignorance to Understanding

The following is an adapted definition of love by M. Scott Peck: *Love is the will to extend one's self for the purpose of nurturing one's own or another's intellectual and spiritual growth.* That definition is packed with meaning.

Love as action. First and foremost, love is an action: "the will to extend one's self." Love requires effort; it is something we do. It is not a feeling that washes over our bodies like the lyrics to a sappy love song. It is how we behave. As such, love is muscular and sinuous and develops through vigorous exercise. To snivel "I'm not *feeling* like I'm in love," should be replaced with the real truth: "I'm not *acting* like I'm in love."

Love directed inward. Love begins at home—with yourself. Love means attending to your own intellectual and spiritual growth. Why? For two reasons:

First, we love ourselves because we are spiritual beings. As such, we have a responsibility to be sensitive to our own sacred selves, to acknowledge and nurture the wisdom that is within us. To ignore or abuse our spiritual selves is equivalent to numbing our minds or starving our bodies.

Second, we attend to our own spiritual growth, because self-love is a prerequisite to offering love to others. We will not extend to others what we do not treasure in ourselves. I have seen this again and again, when counseling couples. Husbands or wives who feel unlovable cannot imagine that another person would love them. So rather than be rejected—their greatest fear—they resort to self-defeating tactics, primarily hostility or depression.

Love directed outward. Love is extended to others. Loving people are deeply interested in the spiritual development of all those they touch—not only their spouses and children, but friends and co-workers as well. Their love is both unconditional and unrestricted. They love because it is the right thing to do, without stipulation or expectation of reciprocity. Moreover, their love has no social or political boundaries; they love indiscriminately. But they are not colorblind (speaking not only of race and nationality, but of gender, religion, and countless affinities), for they cherish the uniqueness and value of all people. Love is not just a pretty word for them; it is an unyielding covenant—a sacred, personal mission: to love without boundaries.

To love is really about moving away from ignorance and toward understanding—understanding of the immeasurable value of self and others. To illustrate, I offer a story that a friend of mine shared about his father. I think it is an astonishing episode that reflects the transformation that can occur when love is allowed in.

All his life, Chester Stoddard never liked black people. Don't ask him why; he just didn't like them. He even gave up watching professional basketball on TV, initially one of his favorite pastimes, because there were too many "black bucks" playing the game. "Ruined the sport," he would lament to his wife, who remained silent, having learned to ignore her husband's ranting over the years.

Chester was now 80 years old. Every Monday at noon he would drive to the Holiday Inn and have lunch with his friends at the Rotary club. Something amazing happened at one of those luncheons. The chapter president stood before the club members and said, "We need one more big brother to sponsor a 16-year-old student. He's a good kid, but, like all kids, he could use some guidance. His name is Tyrone." For some inexplicable reason, Chester raised his hand. "Okay," the president said, "you've got him, Chester."

The next week the old man met Tyrone for the first time in the high school cafeteria after school. Chester arrived first. He sat motionless in a plastic chair, his hands in his lap. His head was down, as if in prayer. He was wondering what he was getting himself into.

"Mr. Stoddard?"

Chester looked up into the black face of a lean, six-foot-two teenager with dreadlocks and a gold earring dangling from his left earlobe.

"Tyrone?" Chester asked tentatively. Not once had it occurred to Chester that the kid might be black. When Chester first heard the name Tyrone, he thought of Tyrone Power dueling with Basil Rathbone in *The Mark of Zorro*. This was all wrong.

"Yeah, that's me," the kid said. He flipped a chair around and straddled it backwards, as quickly and naturally as if it had been choreographed.

"I, uh, I wasn't expecting someone . . . ." Chester stalled.

"Quite so tanned," Tyrone said, flashing a perfect smile. "That's okay. Don't worry about it. I wasn't expecting someone quite so, uh . . ."

"Prehistoric," Chester said, poking fun at himself.

Tyrone smiled and tilted his head, a gesture that said, "Yeah, that about sums it up."

That was the beginning. The two started talking about Tyrone's goals: playing varsity ball (Tyrone had a beautiful pull-up jump shot) and somehow getting through geometry. The more Tyrone spoke, uncommonly relaxed and confident for his years, the more Chester liked the young man. At the end of an hour, it occurred to Chester that he had never before said more than a dozen words to any black person.

The two met once every two weeks for the rest of the school year. Chester actually checked out a book on geometry at the city library. It was a curious sight seeing the old man and the teenager, shoulder to shoulder, hunched over a geometrical enigma. Chester looked forward to their time together; he started shaving extra close on the days he was to meet his young friend. As for Tyrone, he gradually became protective of the old man. Once, when a buddy jibed that his new friend was too old to hold his water, Tyrone stiff-armed the kid and said, "It ain't that way."

Tyrone did make the varsity basketball team that year as a sophomore, and Chester attended every home game. He sat in the section just above the students and cheered until his throat was hoarse. For the first time in years, he was having fun. At the end of the season, Tyrone invited Chester to the team awards' banquet. Chester was proud to accept, and even prouder when Tyrone garnered the rookie-of-the-year award. When Tyrone accepted the small trophy, he pumped it above his head and looked wide-eyed straight at Chester. It was at that moment that Chester knew he loved the young man.

That was three years ago. You can talk to Chester anytime about Tyrone's successes since then. But not on Sunday afternoon; that's the day he watches NBA basketball on TV.

2. The Discipline of Responsibility: From Victimism to Decision-making

I have a Jamaican friend who holds an Olympic silver medal in the mile relay. I asked him how he prepared for such a momentous race.

"I only ran the race once," he said, "but I ran it 10,000 times in my head."

"But what if a competitor had jumped out ahead?" I asked. "Would that have changed your strategy for the race?"

My friend shook his head. "You must run your own race. It does not matter what other runners do. A runner who starts out too fast in the first 200 meters of the race will die in the home stretch. It takes great discipline, but you must always run your own race, just as you practiced in your head."

To run your own race—that simple phrase is for me the essence of responsibility. Responsible people do not fall victim to the strategies of other runners (or harsh circumstances). Rather, they are self-directed—committed to high ideals and the freedom of choice. Unlike victims—who believe that their thoughts, feelings, and behaviors are controlled by outside influences—responsible people (I call them decision-makers) take charge of their lives. They develop a powerful ability to release that which they cannot control, to abide by the teachings expounded in the Alcoholics Anonymous' Prayer of Serenity:

> *Lord, give me the courage to change the things that can and ought to be changed, the serenity to accept the things that cannot be changed, and the wisdom to know the difference.*

The discipline of responsibility is practiced by people who, against all odds, make the right decisions. There are thousands of stories that can be told of such heroic people—political prisoners, rescue teams, freedom fighters, cancer survivors, to name a few. Indeed, each of us may have at least one story to tell from our own experience—a story of courageous responsibility. But none could be more remarkable than the story of Donald Wyman.

In the summer of 1993, Donald Wyman, a woodsman, was clearing wood for a mining company in a remote Pennsylvania forest. A huge tree fell on him, inextricably pinning his left leg. Wyman tried to dig his leg out from under the mammoth tree. It was impossible. He screamed for help for over an hour. Nothing. Finally, with his left leg shattered and bleeding heavily, he made a tourniquet from a rawhide bootlace, tightening it with a chainsaw wrench. Then, incredibly, he set about sawing off his left leg six inches below the knee with a pocketknife. When he had amputated the leg, he crawled to a bulldozer parked 500 feet away, drove it another 2,000 feet to his pickup truck, then drove the truck two miles to a farmhouse. When the farmer telephoned emergency, he described Wyman as "sharp and mentally strong."

A couple of days later, the 37-year-old Wyman spoke at a press conference. "It was a terrible ordeal that I had to get through—being

trapped in the woods like that," he said. "I had a life-and-death situation. And that was my only choice—life or death. I had so much
to live for, I did the only thing I could and chose life." Later, Wyman
said, "Nothing compares to my challenge in the woods. It's all
downhill from now on."

After hearing a story like that, whining about heavy traffic
seems pretty pathetic. Still, Wyman is wrong about one thing. He
did have another choice: he could have chosen death. But
Wyman's response is reflective of all people who apply the discipline of responsibility: a positive, somehow-someway kind of
determination.

If a magic genie were to give me one wish, I would wish for a
double dose of responsibility for every person on earth. Because
with responsibility—the behavior of making right choices, regardless of the situation—nothing is impossible, for, if nothing else, we
could always choose our own attitude.

3. The Discipline of Vision:
From Cynicism to Enthusiasm

The discipline of vision is transformational: It transforms the
individual and the individual's community. It is magical stuff. It
converts raw imagination into noble and revolutionary objectives.
When that happens—when a vision is captured—cynics are transformed into life enthusiasts.

Adversity is the price of admission for being human.
Overcoming adversity is one measure of personal discipline. It is
not always easy. It takes strength, stamina, and ambition—all of
which translates into pain. The enthusiast (a person of vision) is
willing to endure the pain; the cynic is not. Why? Enthusiasts
ungrudgingly pay the price because they are sustained by the
vision of a worthy goal (a happy marriage, a successful career, a
community service well done). Hardships along the way only
enhance the value of the dream. That is why college freshmen submit to the humiliation of hell week: the dream of becoming a
member of an elite fraternity or sorority outstrips the pain of

initiation; for some, the dream is so vivid that the challenges are inconsequential—even fun.

But for cynics, it is a different story. They lack vision. They do not see what could be; they only see what is: the prejudice, the injustice, the chaos. Without a vision to guide them through the maze of adversity, they can never conquer—they can only cope. Their coping skills are an aggregate of neurotic behaviors: criticizing, blaming, angering, and depressing. It is a tragic life philosophy.

A vision is both noble—congruent with principles of integrity—and revolutionary. It must stand for truth, despite popular or conventional opinion.

History offers many inspirational visionaries, including John Kennedy and his "impossible" mission of putting a man on the moon and returning him home safely, and Nelson Mandela and his revolutionary dream of putting an end to apartheid in South Africa. But my favorite is Woodrow Wilson, president during World War I. Repeatedly, Wilson fought against popular opinion, particularly the allies' insistence on dividing the spoils of war (their greed and malice set the stage for World War II). Despite sickness and exhaustion, Wilson boldly campaigned for his Fourteen Points—"open covenants of peace, openly arrived at"—and the League of Nations. In the end, Wilson was defeated (the crippled League of Nations dissolved in 1946), but his work set the foundation for the United Nations—still, despite its imperfections, our best hope for a world made "safe for democracy."

The discipline of vision is available to anyone—regardless of position—who is willing to transform imagination into even modest dreams of nobility and revolution. I share three examples:

• Deanna is my wife's cousin. Three years ago she spoke to us for the first time in 30 years. It was not that she had been holding a grudge—we had just drifted apart, the way people do when they are caught up in the urgency of making a living. I did not know Deanna at all, so when she telephoned, I was less than effervescent.

"I'm Nita's cousin," Deanna explained.

"Uh-huh."

"I want to meet you," she said. "You see, I've decided that family is important. I want to know my family."

I was about to say, "Well, isn't that nice," when Deanna pressed on. "So," she said, "my husband and I are coming to see you. We'll be there on Friday, about 4 o'clock in the afternoon."

Before I could say, "But I don't know you," I was listening to a dial tone.

Two days later Deanna showed up at our doorstep, as promised. She didn't just introduce herself; she kicked off an entire stage show. In the first 30 minutes, Deanna shared comical and revealing episodes from her life story. From anyone else, the production would have detonated intimacy overload, but from Deanna it was—in a strange, Busby Berkeley sort of way—endearing. By the time Deanna closed the show two days later, I was, yes, gasping for air, but irrevocably in love with the girl. From that moment on Deanna became one of our best friends.

Deanna had a noble vision (to know family), and she did it in a revolutionary way. I admire her for the clarity of her vision.

• I also admire my new friend, Jamie. I have been impressed by the intensity of his personal vision. Jamie knew early on that he wanted to help people adopt healthy lifestyles—that was his calling. His training in psychotherapy was typical: a sampling of psychoanalysis, behaviorism, and cognitive therapy. He tried these treatments, but they didn't feel right to Jamie. He found that his clients made little progress, even after months of intensive therapy.

So Jamie began to experiment. Little by little he developed a treatment he called "dramedy." With a natural comedic and dramatic flair, Jamie invited his clients to describe their current state of affairs. Then, together, counselor and client would create dramatic scenarios that depicted past injuries and, more importantly, future successes. The results were startling. Clients who had succumbed to years of life-threatening addictions were now choosing, for the first time in their lives, to be clean and sober.

Jamie's treatment isn't based on conventional wisdom. In his own way he is a revolutionary, fighting an uphill battle for a noble cause. He has not been lauded by more traditional practitioners (in fact, in some cases he has been dismissed as misguided), but for Jamie none of that matters. He is having success and fulfilling his vision of helping others choose health over sickness, life over death.

- Finally, I will tell you about Hugh and Fritzi Johnson. My wife and I met them during a two-year teaching experience in Algeria. The Johnson's vision was to serve the Berbers of Algeria, who had been ravaged by Algeria's eight-year struggle for independence from the French. The war, finally ending with Algeria's declaration of independence in 1962, was horrifically bloody—culminating in 100,000 French and one million Algerian causalities. After the cease-fire, an additional 150,000 pro-French Muslims were killed by the Algerian National Liberation Front.

With that as a backdrop, Hugh and Fritzi established a mission in a small Berber village. Hugh learned to speak French, Arabic, and Berber. He served in whatever way he could. When the French fled Algeria, they took with them all of the country's skilled labor. Algeria was in desperate need of educators, so Hugh and Fritzi spent much of their time teaching language to the Berber children. The Johnsons' devotion to the people of Algeria was so renown that they and their two daughters were always protected from national terrorists during frequent coups d'état.

What a noble and revolutionary vision: to serve the impoverished and war-torn Berbers, when the mere color of their skin could have easily marked them as an enemy of the people.

Vision precedes every noble behavior. The people I have mentioned in this section are people of vision. Obviously, I could not talk about their vision (internal pictures) without talking about their behavior (external actions)—the two go hand-in-hand. Certainly, there are those who do not take action on their visions (we call them dreamers)—and they must live with their forsaken dreams. The real heroes are those who act on their visions by exercising the next discipline of personal effectiveness: the discipline of commitment.

4. The Discipline of Commitment:
From Bystanding to Participation

The discipline of commitment is the steadfast and deliberate action of converting vision into reality. It is the natural consequence of responsibility and vision. It is easy to be committed when we have made the responsible decision to be swept up by a noble and revolutionary objective; deliberate action inevitably follows. Conversely, without the foundation of responsibility and vision, one becomes a bystander—huddled meekly in the last row of the balcony, dispassionately watching the show open and close. If bystanders have a vision (it's hard to tell), it is squelched by the fear of failure or rejection. Suppressing vision contradicts human instinct; bystanders cope with that incongruence by consciously or subconsciously diminishing the importance of the vision. Ultimately, in the most extreme cases, the self-deception leads to lives that are tragically void of passion.

On the other end of the continuum are the participators—those who are acting on their dreams. These people are particularly committed to truth and importance. What do I mean by that?

First, participators are committed to discovering personal truth: the far reaches of their talents, the nature of their mission. They want to know what it means to live a life of 100-percent integrity—what it means to be a spiritual being. These are tough issues and seldom fully understood, even in a lifetime, but—and this point is central—the people who are well schooled in the discipline of commitment are closer to knowing the full truth.

Second, participators attend to what is supremely important in their lives: namely, a sense of mission and devotion to relationships. They are impatient with the trivial. Instead, they continually ask, "What is the most important thing we can do this moment to help us move closer to our purpose?" Fueled by responsibility and vision, these participators demonstrate their commitment by zeroing in on high-leverage, mission-oriented activities.

Bill and Kathy Magee know all about the discipline of commitment. They have taken their vision and turned it into 50,000 smiles. Bill Magee is a plastic surgeon, and his wife Kathy is a nurse. They have the dream of giving smiles to thousands of children around the world who suffer from cleft lip, cleft palate, or other birth disfigurements. In 1982, the Magees founded Operation Smile, a nonprofit organization that boasts 24 chapters in 11 U.S. cities and 46 locations in 19 countries.

Operating strictly from donated medical services, Dr. Magee leads the way by donating 150 surgical days a year (he has never taken one nickel in salary). For 20 weeks each year, he travels to any of 18 underdeveloped countries to operate on patients who would not otherwise be treated.

The Magees' dream was first ignited in 1981 when they volunteered to join a medical team on a five-day mission to the Philippines. Dr. Magee's assignment was to operate on children with cleft lips and cleft palates. It was an emotional experience. "People pushed their babies at us," Kathy said, "tugged at our sleeves, and begged us to help their children." But after putting in 16-hour shifts, the doctors were forced to leave 250 patients untreated. The Magees made a promise to themselves to return the following year. They did just that—with an 18-member team of their own: Operation Smile. The Magees have never looked back. In 1999 alone, 3,000 medical volunteers traveled to 18 countries around the world—Nicaragua, Brazil, Columbia, Kenya, Thailand, to name a few—and created 5,300 new smiles.

More inspirational than sheer numbers are the stories, like that of Angel Dias, an 18-year-old Nicaraguan boy with a cleft lip. Angel had never been to school and could not read or write. He was an outcast in his own family: virtually ignored at Christmas and (what hurt him most) never kissed by his father.

Angel had heard that Dr. Magee was in Managua. The teenager decided to act on his dream. "He borrowed $30 from his neighbor," Magee recounts, "rode a donkey for hours down the mountain from his village, spent two days on a river boat, then rode a bus for another day." In all, Angel traveled 250 miles to find the doctor of miracles.

Angel's smile was restored in a standard 45-minute operation. Afterwards, the Nicaraguan government provided an army
helicopter to return Angel to a town close to his mountain village.
Dr. Magee accompanied his patient. The mayor of the town
agreed to take care of Angel until the boy was strong enough to
make the 12-hour donkey ride back to his village. The last thing
Dr. Magee asked Angel was what he wanted to do when he
returned home. The boy looked at the doctor and smiled: "I'm
going to kiss my father."

Bill and Kathy Magee understand that vision without action is
meaningless. They also understand that the action that is most
rewarding transcends self-interest—the heart of the fifth discipline.

5. The Discipline of Service: From Egoist to Altruist

When we enter the world as infants, we arrive completely self-
serving. We are the ultimate egoists, certain that the world was created for the sole purpose of making us happy. That is not a
criticism, only an observation. Infants have no understanding of
social mores and should not be condemned for their ignorance.
However, if they are raised by loving parents, children mature—
they grow intellectually, socially, and spiritually—and become
increasingly altruistic. They become less concerned with themselves and more concerned with the welfare of others. That is what
it means to be immersed in the discipline of service.

At least, that is what is supposed to happen. Unfortunately,
altruism doesn't always win out. Often we get caught up in the
spin of ego, working hard to prove we are important and deserving of special treatment. We don't want 15 minutes of fame; we
want a lifetime of fame, or at least a good measure of adoration.
And, perhaps more than anything, we want others to know that
we are right. All that posturing is the egoist speaking.

Altruists, on the other hand, have nothing to prove. They operate not from ego, but from spirit. They only want to make a contribution—to make a positive difference in the lives of others. They are
interested in leading communities—families, teams, organizations,

cities, countries, even the world—to a better place. Like the Magees, they want to be of service.

Understanding the difference between egoists and altruists is very important, and deserves an example:

Once when I was flying across the country on business, the woman seated next to me was crocheting. After a while, she said, "I do love to fly."

"Oh?"

"Yes, indeed. To think that one could be anywhere in the world in less than a day—it's astonishing."

"I take it you've done a fair amount of traveling?" I asked.

"Oh, my, my, my," she said.

I took it that my question was the understatement of the millennium—the old millennium. The woman went on to tell me about her adventures. She was particularly fond of Dunoon.

"And where is Dunoon?" I asked innocently enough.

She never looked up from her crocheting. "Why, it's *still* in Scotland, of course," she said.

Hmph. So that's the way it was going to be. I narrowed my gaze and quickly devised a plan to get even. Now, as providence would have it, I was raised in a quiet town in Southeastern Washington called Pasco. It's a wonderful community, but not exactly a household word when it comes to world geography. So I'm thinking, I'll ask her if she knows where Pasco is. And she'll say, "No I don't." And then, I'll level her with my killer line: "Well, then we're even, aren't we?" (Operating from the ego is never a proud moment.)

So, I said, "Well, tell me, do you know where Pasco is?"

And she said, "Do you mean Pasco, Washington, or Pasco, Peru?"

Later I looked it up—there is a Pasco, Peru. Arrrgh. But, you know what? It serves me right. I was operating from ego. If I had been operating from an altruistic spirit, I would have simply said, "Oh, I didn't know that. Tell me more."

Obviously, living in the spirit all the time is not easy. I struggle with it constantly. On that day, I flew 2,000 miles, side-by-side with the crochet lady in absolute silence—except for the small voice in my head that was whispering, "Allen, you lived for two years in a little mountain village in Algeria. Why didn't you say Larbaa Nath Irathen?"

Of course, all that negative ego talk did nothing for me, nothing for the crochet lady, and nothing to ease the boredom of reading for the nth time several passages from the in-flight shopping catalog.

To make the transition from ego to altruism is a giant leap in maturity. Some never make it. For those who do, it usually comes in mid-life, during their forties and fifties. I enjoy the analogy that Bob Buford applies in his book, *Half Time*. Buford explains that life is like a football game. In the first half of the game, we are intent on racking up the score. We want to climb the ladder of success, to be seen as bright and powerful and important. (It sounds like ego, doesn't it?) And then there is half time. At half time, the players go to the locker room and try to figure out what happened in the first half of the game and determine what needs to happen in the second half.

Many people get stuck in the first half (struggling until their last breath to make a name for themselves) or in half time (scratching their heads, trying to figure out what to do next). The most effective players go on to the second half of the game. They make a shift, as Buford puts it, from *success* to *significance*. They seek a lifestyle that is replete with meaning, one that leaves a legacy of love, peace, forgiveness, and wisdom—a lifestyle of service.

The human body is an amalgam of systems—cardiovascular, pulmonary, neurological, musculoskeletal, and more. Each of these systems, by its own right, is amazing, but working together, the merger of systems is simply miraculous. The same may be said of the five disciplines. A person who hones all five disciplines—who loves unconditionally, acts responsibly, envisions deliberately, commits wholeheartedly, and serves without expectations of praise or reciprocity—is a person of astonishing power. How we get there is the subject of the next chapter.

Chapter 3

HE MEANS

AWAKENING THE FIVE DISCIPLINES OF EFFECTIVENESS

The changes in our life must come from the impossibility to live otherwise than according to the demands of our conscience. . . not from our mental resolution to try a new form of life.

—Leo Tolstoy

Defining discipline is one thing; applying it is something else. Some people seem to flow naturally into a life of discipline—usually the descendants of disciplined parents or grandparents. But, more often than not, practicing discipline is a tussle. We know its good for us—usually there's no argument there—we just don't like the idea of applying it. When pressed to explain, we draw from a worn file of excuses—many defying any semblance of logic: "it's too hard; it's not my style; it's arrogant."

And, yet, discipline can be awakened and employed. If that were not true, we would still be cooking our dinners on the end of a sharp stick. Progress only comes through discipline. Fortunately, discipline may be awakened through euphoric and traumatic epiphanies. For instance, consider my young friend, Jonathan, who is currently a college freshman. He likes to put in what he calls "all-nighters," cramming for the test to come on the following day. As much as I love the kid, he is currently in the process of getting an education in cramming—and not an education in biology, English, or history. There has been no awakening—at least not yet.

If Jonathan is lucky, he will be awakened to the enduring rewards of discipline though a euphoric or traumatic epiphany. For example, one day in biology class, my young friend may be suddenly swept away by, say, the intriguing mystery of physiology or genetics or paleontology. That euphoric epiphany could send him scrambling to the science library for research (okay, not likely, but it could happen). Or, he could receive a "D" on the biology mid-term exam and, remembering the conditions of his father's financial graces, get singularly serious about his studies—a traumatic epiphany.

The dictionary defines an *epiphany* as "a sudden, intuitive revelation." That is often the case—an unexpected illness or death in the family can certainly produce a sudden epiphany. But, in the context of this discussion, an epiphany is expanded to include both gradual and instant revelations, for often understanding is revealed slowly—as in the gradual awareness of parenthood or the ongoing understanding of romantic love.

Let's take a closer look at the two types of epiphanies.

TRAUMATIC EPIPHANIES

A traumatic epiphany is a disturbing event—almost always caused by unapplied human competencies and insufficient discipline—resulting in increased awareness and a strong desire to disassociate from the activating event. The disturbing event for my friend, Jonathan, was the "D" in biology and the potential loss of financial support. The low mark was no accident; it was the product of too little discipline. That disturbing event served as a wakeup call, resulting in a renewed interest in study.

The fact that disturbing events are almost always self-inflected should be underscored. There are very few "accidents."

Automobile accidents are invariably caused by drivers who are inattentive, reckless, or intoxicated. Divorce is the product of too little love. Even sickness is often symptomatic of poor diet, insufficient exercise, and diluted stress management skills. Acts of nature excluded, traumatic epiphanies do not just happen to us; we choose them—as demonstrated by the following example. I share this very personal story with my father's blessings, in *our* hope that it might create a flash of insight for someone else.

It is late at night. I am in bed, the blanket over my ears, trying to shut out the profane scent and sound of a "stranger" in the house: the commotion of my drunken father crashing through the front door and the argument that invariably ensued between my mother and my father. I dared not stir from my bed.

The next morning, my father would gather the family around the kitchen table and say, "I'm going to change. I'm not going to drink anymore. I'm sorry. Please forgive me."

We had heard it all before. I said nothing. I stared blankly at the kitchen tabletop and promised that I would not be like my father in that way: I would never drink.

My father would be dry for a few weeks, maybe a few months, and then it would happen again. And, predictably, he would gather the family around the kitchen table for his speech of atonement. I could not, would not, forgive him.

Years later—when my brother and I were fully grown and living away from home—my father drove out of town on business one weekend. Although he was 125 miles from home, he decided to have a drink at a friend's house before heading back. One drink lead to another and another. Soon both men were drunk.

Dad staggered out of the house and into his car and somehow managed to drive onto the freeway. But he was swerving all over the road. A policeman spotted him and pulled him over.

Dad spent the night in jail. He was photographed, fingerprinted, and thrown in the "drunk tank." It was a humiliation beyond anything he had ever experienced. The next morning he appeared before the judge and defended himself.

"Judge," he said, "I believe I have a purpose for my life. This drunken behavior is not that purpose. I have disgraced your city, my family, and my God. I am embarrassed and ashamed of myself. I pledge to you that this will never, ever happen again. For the first time in my life, I know that I am an alcoholic. For the first time in my life, I know that I cannot drink again.

"I do not know what punishment you have for me. Whatever it is, I am willing to take it and more. From this moment on, my life is changed."

And Dad's life did change. That transformational event occurred 22 years ago; he has not had a drink since.

My dad did it the hard way. His awakening came by way of a traumatic epiphany—a change motivated by the intense wish to decrease the pain. Do not misunderstand: I applaud my dad's victory. There is, however, a more effective way of changing that is driven not by the avoidance of pain but by the attraction of joy. It is called an *euphoric epiphany* and is the subject of the next section.

Euphoric Epiphanies

A euphoric epiphany is a pleasurable event—caused by applied human competencies and sufficient discipline—resulting in increased awareness and a strong desire to associate with the activating event. I often experience a small euphoric epiphany when I deliver a winning presentation. The speech did not appear by magic; it was developed by tapping the five human competencies and associated disciplines. There is an afterglow that follows a successful presentation that compels me to repeat the activity. Basically, I am addicted to the joy.

Euphoric epiphanies turn cynics into enthusiasts and bystanders into participants. For that reason, we ought to actively create opportunities for epiphanies. We should constantly tantalize our senses—transforming life into a cavalcade of excursions into unknown territory. We need to read more, travel more, make new friends, and visit old pals. We need to experiment and explore and get up in the morning with a new adventure in mind. We need to fill up our senses, because experience begets euphoric epiphanies, which begets discipline, which begets enduring joy and peace of mind.

I am smiling now, just thinking about all of the euphoric epiphanies of my life: the day I directed the 6th grade band in a cacophonous rendition of *Silent Night* at the all-school Christmas concert; the curtain call of my first high school one-act play; my introduction to the poetic prose of D. H. Lawrence; strolling hand-in-hand with my wife Nita along the canals of Venice; standing awestruck at Panhandle Gap on the Wonderland Trail, overlooking the majesty of Mount Rainier. These experiences (and many, many more) have done something magical: They have taken the strain out of discipline, for *discipline naturally emanates from the joy of experience.*

All euphoric epiphanies tap one or more of the five human competencies (and associated disciplines). The epiphany is particularly powerful when all five competencies are incorporated into the experience, as the following example illustrates.

It was Father's Day. Driving home from work, I began to think about my dad. At first I flashed on my childhood memories—the smell of alcohol on my father's breath—and then I thought, "Allen, what are you doing? Your father has been sober for 15 years. How long are you going to savor those memories?"

That was a moment of *insight* for me. I became aware that I had carried my resentment long enough. I also heard the voice of *moral knowledge*—a voice that said it was time for forgiveness. Through my *imagination*, I began to create a movie in my head. I saw myself driving to my father's home (he lives nearby, in the town just across the river), walking to the front door, knocking, being greeted, sitting down in the chair by the door, and talking.

I did just that. I acted on my *independent will* and drove my car along the interstate that crosses the river to where my father lives. Just as I had imagined, my father greeted me at the door.

"Hey, Son. Look who's here," he said over his shoulder to my mother. "Come on in."

I sat down in the chair next to the door and, tapping the competency of *self-transcendence* and the discipline of service, I began the process of seeking forgiveness.

I leaned forward in the chair. "Dad, I've been thinking about you today."

"Uh-oh," my dad said with a wry smile. "What have I done wrong now?"

Although his question was offered in good humor, it was not without meaning. Dad had thought of himself as the black sheep of the family for as long as I could remember—and, of course, I had played my part in keeping him tethered to that role.

"Dad," I said, "It's not about what you have done *wrong*, but about what you have done *right*."

I saw my father's shoulders relax. He settled deeper into his chair.

"Tell me, Dad, how long have you been sober?"

Dad smiled. "Fifteen years," he announced, snapping a little nod to accent his words.

"Dad, I have never told you how proud I am of you for that achievement."

"Thank you, Son."

"And I want you to know," my voice getting softer now, "that I forgive you for the hurt that I felt as a child."

"Thank you, Son."

"But, more importantly, I hope you will forgive me for waiting this long to do this."

My father said nothing. He lifted himself out of the chair and walked toward me.

I stood up and met him in the center of the living room. He wrapped his arms around me and gave me one of the longest, sweetest hugs I've ever had.

As I was enveloped in my father's arms, I looked at my mother sitting quietly in her favorite chair. With tears streaming down her cheeks, she radiated the smile of an angel; it was the look of one who, after 10,000 prayers, had finally been relieved of her duties as family peacemaker.

How did that moment of forgiveness happen? Through the application of the five human competencies and associated disciplines. It was a euphoric epiphany—an unforgettable and joyful turning point for my father and me. We have never looked back.

TESTING THE FIVE HIGHER-ORDER HUMAN COMPETENCIES

I suggest that you test the legitimacy of the five human competencies (and their associated disciplines). Think about a vital personal or professional relationship that is frustrating you—a relationship that you know is not right. With that case in mind, consider the open-ended statements below.

As you complete the statements, monitor your feelings. Do you feel at peace with your responses? If not, try again; you probably have not yet tapped your higher self. If you do feel a sense of peace, take action: seek reconciliation, forgiveness, and peace.

Do I guarantee success? No. Where other people are concerned, I can make no guarantees, but I can say this: If you are operating fully from your higher self, you will feel a sense of peace—and, after that, you will be best served by releasing that which you cannot control.

1. *Insight.* The other person's behavior aside, the things I am doing to help block the resolution of this issue are . . .

2. *Moral knowledge.* As I listen to my heart in this situation, I know I should . . .

3. *Imagination.* As I visualize the healing of this relationship, I see myself . . .

4. *Independent will.* The steps I will take to realize my vision are . . .

5. *Self-transcendence.* My action will promote love, peace, forgiveness, or service by . . .

Chapter 4

THE RESULTS

THE LEGACY OF DISCIPLINE

We have no more right to consume happiness without producing it than to consume wealth without producing it.

—George Bernard Shaw

Character is the basis of happiness, and happiness the sanction of character.

—George Santayana

I ona was just about the unhappiest person I have ever met. The first time I heard her voice was when she called to make an appointment to discuss her relationship with her husband. She did not sound depressed or anxious—in fact, she sounded somewhat confident. After a few minutes of dialogue, we agreed to meet the following week.

On the day of the appointment, I greeted Iona at the door. She was a tall, thin woman in her late forties. Although her eyes darted about the room, she seemed quite at home—almost cavalier. Still, she did not extend her hand, and I, in deference, did not offer mine.

"I don't know if you can help me, Dr. Johnson," she said, as she sat down in the big leather chair in my office. As she spoke, she tapped the lid of an ordinary shoebox that was perched on her lap. "I don't know if you can help me at all."

"You're probably right about that," I said, "but I bet you can help yourself. What brings you here?"

This is a question that I greatly prefer over "How can I help you?"—a phrase that denotes a relationship of dependency.

"Well, let me tell you," she said, as she lifted the lid of the shoebox.

I saw immediately that the box was filled with ragged scraps of paper, each no bigger than the palm of her hand. The box was so crammed with these paper snippets that they puffed up like baked bread when she lifted the lid.

Iona selected at random one of the pieces of paper at the top of the heap. She held the paper with both hands. "Today, my husband tweaked my ear at the dinner table," she read.

She gently bedded the paper into the box and selected another snippet. Again she held the paper fragment with both hands. "Today, my husband called me a foul name in front of company."

I was becoming more and more intrigued.

Iona rummaged though the scraps of paper and seized a jagged piece of fabric. She waved the piece of cloth like a small flag of surrender. "This is a piece of material from my favorite dress that my husband tore."

She delicately replaced the swatch of fabric and, next, fished out an audio cassette tape. "Do you have a recorder?" she asked.

"Yes, I do," I said. I plugged in a portable recorder, inserted Iona's tape, and pushed the *play* button. It was a recording of a bitter argument—secretly recorded, I was to learn later—between Iona and her husband. I listened for 10 or 15 minutes, until I could take it no more. (About 15 minutes is my threshold of tolerance when it comes to listening to misery.) I stopped the tape.

"Wow," I said, "this is incredible." Did all this happen in the last week or so?"

Iona shook her head. "No. This happened in 1972," she said, recovering the first piece of paper. "And this"—the second piece in hand—"happened in 1964. And this . . . ."

"Oh, my," I said. Despite my years of training in counseling, it was difficult to disguise my judgment of Iona. "I'll tell you what," I said after a long pause. "It must be painful carrying around all those ancient wounds. What do you say we have a little ceremony and burn them?"

For the first time, Iona made direct eye contact. She smiled demurely and said, "Thank you, Dr. Johnson, for your time." With that, she placed the lid on the shoebox, stood, held the box close to her chest, and walked to the door. She disappeared before I knew what had happened.

Many years have passed since that disturbing visit, and I am sad to report that I have not seen Iona since. She was a woman who had a Ph.D. in misery. Her very identity was wrapped up in her unhappiness. She collected heartache like other people collect stamps or rare coins. She took great delight in sharing her collection with anyone who was willing to listen—particularly with people schooled in the art of recognizing misery. But Iona did not sell or trade her misery; she was only a buyer. And this is the tragedy of it all: Her collection became, for her, too beloved to discard.

I am sure that Iona believed that her misery was outside of her control, that it pierced her like a bullet in a drive-by shooting—for, after all, she had a box full of misery to prove it. The fact is, Iona did have control of her life; she did make her own choices—she simply chose misery.

When I tell this story, people tend to chuckle, as if to say, "My, my, isn't that a silly way to behave." But, guess what? All of us carry a shoebox with us; ours are just neatly tucked away in the crevasses of our minds and hearts, where they can't be seen.

In the end we all have to ask, "What snippets of misery do we choose to collect and protect with a kind of holy righteousness?" For it is strange, indeed, that we should argue so vehemently for our own misery.

• • •

Discipline has its payoff: enduring joy. That was my hypothesis when I began to look into the nature of discipline; what I discovered confirmed my intuition.

I began my quest to understand the connection between happiness and discipline by designing an 18-item personal assessment to correlate one's sense of well-being (peace, happiness, and anticipation for the new day) to one's state of total discipline (love, responsibility, vision, commitment, and service).

I then sampled two populations: business adults and teenage students. The findings pertaining to business adults are the subject of this chapter.[1]

THE CORRELATION BETWEEN
DISCIPLINE AND WELL-BEING

My research shows that a sense of well-being—for both teenagers and adults—positively correlates with personal discipline. In fact, the correlation is so strong that there is less than one chance in 10,000 that the results are derived in error.

What does that mean? *If you want to be happy, get disciplined.* That is the bottom line. People who are, by their own admission, the most content are also, by their own admission, the most disciplined.

My research findings overwhelmingly support the premise of this book: *Enduring joy is not something that is sprinkled on you like holy water—it is something that you do.* Happy people are extravagant doers: they are voracious learners (love), creators of their own destiny (responsibility), diligent planners (vision), champions of balance in their personal and professional lives (commitment), and stalwarts of kindness (service). These people do not whine about their condition. They certainly do not collect their misery in a treasured shoebox; they exploit their condition by turning even meager resources into their advantage. These are the kind of people that you want to have over for dinner; you can be sure that their conversation would be upbeat in content and kind in spirit.

[1] The 18-item profile designed to assess personal discipline, along with a detailed statistical analysis of the results—for both teenagers and adults—may be found on my website: http://members.theglobe.com/allenjohnson/go.

HAPPY VERSUS UNHAPPY ADULTS

What makes the difference between adults who are happy and those who are miserable? To discover the answer, I compared the scores of adults who scored in the top 25 percent bracket on well-being (the happy people) against those who scored in the bottom 25 percent of well-being (the unhappy people). Then I asked this question: How do these two groups differ when it comes to discipline? I found four interesting results.

Happy adults know who they want to be. The greatest difference between happy and unhappy people has to do with the clarity of their vision: happy adults have a clear picture of who they want to be. These people have a *mission* for themselves, some even refer to it as a *calling*. They have found their place in the world, or at least the path that leads to their life's destination. They not only know who they want to be, they also know what they want to accomplish.

In contrast, unhappy people are aimless. They wander from project to project, job to job, without any enduring sense of belonging. They feel out of sorts—restless with their place in the world. Talking to these people is like talking to a bewildered 13-year-old.

"So tell me, where do you hope to be in five years?"
"I dunno."
"Oh, you must have some idea. Give it a shot."
"I suppose I'll be doing pretty much what I'm doing now."
"And what's that?"
"I dunno. Nothing much."

Visionary adults know exactly where they are going (and when there is a bend in the river—a marriage, a birth, a death, a layoff—they simply set a new course).

Visualization has been the subject of research in pain and cancer clinics around the country for years. There is impressive evidence to suggest that some patients can arrest and even reverse their medical condition through mental imagery. If so, if we can alter the chemistry within our bodies, don't you think we are capable of altering the course of our lives? The most mature adults not only *think* they can (vision), but *prove* it by whacking out a path through the jungle of uncertainty (commitment).

Happy adults are balanced. Adults who are most happy recognize what is important in their lives and work hard to keep all things—their personal and professional lives—in balance. Their balance does not come by accident; they plan what they want to accomplish each week.

Those who are unhappy live lives that are out of balance. After talking to hundreds of people on this subject, I have found that the more unhappy people are, the more they are likely to have placed their personal lives at risk by focusing entirely on their careers. The outcome of an interview with these people becomes predictable:

"How do you feel about your life these days?"
"I have to admit, I'm struggling."
"What's going on?"
"I'm putting in too many damn hours at work."
"Is that affecting your home life?"
"What home life? Do I have a home?"
"Sounds like an unhappy situation. So, what are you doing to change things?"
"There's nothing much I can do."
"I see. Well, how about this: How much time do you spend planning your week?"
"Come on, get real. Who has time for that? Besides I know what I have to do; I don't have to write it down."
[*Unspoken thought.*] "Evidently not."

Most adults, particularly young adults, knock themselves out to make a name for themselves. They claim, "It's the price of getting ahead in business." That may be so, but it is also—far too often— the price of losing touch with family and personal passions.

I determined early in my career not to let that happen. My philosophy was based on the importance of personal balance: of creating a place for myself in business, yes, but also in being careful to maintain *relationships* (particularly with my wife), while pursuing creative passions (writing, painting, entertaining, playing piano) and outdoor adventures (bicycling, mountain climbing, scuba diving). To that end (and I know what I am about to say will sound inconceivable, if not crazy, to some people) I made it clear to past employers that I would not work more than 40 hours a week.

"I never heard of such a thing," a manager once told me. "Nobody puts a limit on how many hours he works."

"I do," I said, holding my ground.

Was my decision *career limiting*? Maybe. But a more important question is this: Was my decision *life expanding*? The answer is an unequivocal "yes."

Happy adults are calm. Happy people are able to release the frustrating situations that are outside their control. They are able to say: "I don't particularly like this, but there's nothing that I can do about it—I just have to let it go." That's a liberating position; it enables these people to spend their time working on the things that they can control.

In contrast, the unhappy adults don't forget a thing. It rankles them that others get away with murder (it may rankle the happy people as well, but they don't obsess about it). The unhappy adults waste a great deal of energy complaining and criticizing. They hold on to grudges with relish. They tend to be quick to gossip and unmerciful in confessing the sins of others. Talking to them is frustrating because their premise is also their conclusion: *The world is a scary place, and people are out to get you.* The conversation goes something like this:

"How do you feel about where you are at this point in your life?"
"I can't get ahead."
"Oh, why is that?"
"*They* won't let me get ahead."

"What do you mean?"

"You know what I mean. Unless you belong to the good ol' boys' club, you've got zero chance of getting anywhere in the company."

"Oh?"

"Just look around. All the VP's are golfing buddies."

"Could you be a golfing buddy?"

"Sure, like I could afford to run around with that crew. You don't get it, do you? They don't want you as their buddy; they want you in your place."

Yes, there may be truth to the client's complaints (there are people who cling to power like a spoiled child). But mature adults don't fret over the behavior of others. If there is any fretting to be done, it is over their own behavior: meaning they are more concerned about doing the right thing than they are about fixing others. This attitude is very liberating.

Releasing frustrating situations—particularly if you believe that you have been attacked, victimized, or unjustly accused or characterized—does not come instinctively. In fact, our instinct is to counterattack. But when we choose to step away from insult and injury, we exhibit the most courageous acts of humankind. Curiously, as I was writing this chapter, a telephone call reminded me of this truth.

I could tell in the first five seconds that it was a telephone marketing call. When I receive such calls, my usual response is to say I am not interested and immediately hang up; the whole exchange takes less than 10 seconds (I figure my abruptness is best for the caller and me). This time, for some reason, I decided to try a new approach:

"Hello, Mr. Johnson, how are you?" the caller asked.

"I'm fine," I said. "And how are you? How's your family?"

There was a small laugh on the other end. "Not so good."

"Oh? What's going on?" I asked.

"My mother-in-law did something very cruel, very hateful."

"Uh-oh," I said softly. "So what are you going to do about it?"

Another small laugh. "It's not what *I'm* going to do. It's what *she's* going to do."

"So, she's the one who committed the sin. And it's her duty to seek your forgiveness. Is that it?"

"Right."

"So how long are you going to wait for that to happen?"

"What do you mean?"

"I mean you could be waiting a lifetime."

Silence.

I went on. "I know it's tough, but you may have to take the first step to reconciliation."

"Yeah, I know. It's what I've got to do. It also involves my daughter."

"Wow. So now the resentment is intergenerational," I said.

"Yeah."

"Can you allow that to happen?"

"No, not really."

There was a pause.

"This has been an incredible conversation," the caller said. "Thanks."

"That's okay."

I waited for the caller to hang up. He did not. After a pause he asked, "So what do you do?"

"I'm a psychologist."

"Have you written any books."

"Yes, I have."

"Could they help me with . . . how should I say?"

"Resolving family conflict?" I offered.

"Exactly," the caller said.

"Sure," I said. "I have a new book coming out soon entitled *The Power Within*. You might want to read it."

"Cool. I'll buy it and read it. Thanks and goodbye."

"Hey, wait a minute," I said. "Don't you want to sell me something?"

"Nah, not this time."

"Okay," I said. "Good luck to you." And then I added quickly, "Hey, regarding your family—do the right thing."

"I will," the caller said. "I definitely will."

I don't expect to hear from the caller again, but I hope he has done the right thing. It would be a spectacular act of courage.

Happy adults are spiritual. Happy people make an effort to grow spiritually. I suggest that the happier people are, the more likely they are to look beyond themselves. They recognize that they are spiritual beings and, as such, are responsible for seeking greater understanding of the wonder of life. The more they strive to understand, the more they are drawn to the idea of making a contribution. Truly spiritual people tend to be more other-centered.

The unhappy people are more capricious about their spiritual lives. They tend to be more egocentric, concerned about their personal wealth and rank in life. They keep score—making certain that others recognize their brilliance. For myself, I tend to grow weary of conversations with those whose spiritual lives have been abandoned or ignored.

"What is most important to you?"

"To make money."

"Anything else?"

"To make a truckload of money."

"Well, okay, but is that all there is?"

Recently, a good and longtime friend of mine died. His name was Harvey Hart. A couple of days before his death, I visited him in the hospital. He was unable to speak, but I think—I want to believe—that he recognized me. I bent over my old friend and whispered in his ear, "I love you, Harvey." They were words that I had never spoken to him before. Then I looked at him, and I think I saw a hint of a smile—I'm almost sure I did.

A couple of weeks later, after the funeral, I visited Harvey's wife, Ida. I told her that story. And then I said, "I'm not taking any chances, Ida. I want to go on record right now: I love you."

Ida began to cry, and I thought, "Why have I waited so long?"

I tell that story because I believe that saying "I love you" (in every way possible) may be as close as we get to becoming spiritual beings. What will it take for us to learn: Life is not about *stuff*; it is about *relationships*.

A COMPARISON OF OLDER VERSUS YOUNGER ADULTS

According to my research, older adults (ages 51 to 85) are happier and more disciplined than younger adults (ages 20 to 35). On average, older adults score significantly higher than younger adults on well-being and total discipline.

Older adults are more spiritual. The most distinct difference between older and younger adults has to do with their spiritual lives. Older adults are clearly more concerned with their spiritual development. They tend to be more vigilant about doing the right thing: helping others grow, doing what is truly important, remaining at peace—even when others are unkind.

What causes that transition from self-centeredness to other-centeredness? What is it about growing older that creates within us a spiritual orientation?

I put those questions to a 69-year-old friend of mine, Jack, a retired Air Force fighter pilot who flew 53 missions during the Korean War and two tours in Vietnam. I like Jack very much; there is a quiet peace and wisdom about him that is absorbing. I have a hunch that he raised hell as a kid and learned a thing or two while he was at it. This is what he had to say on the subject:

"As you get older you learn to maintain a better balance."

"What do you mean by that?" I asked.

"When you're younger, you're concerned with making a living, raising kids, obtaining goals."

"Proving yourself," I suggested.

"Yes, that's part of it too," Jack said. "But then a change occurs—a change in inner flow. There is a shift in what is important. When you're young you want to have fun; it's a self-interest thing. As you get older, you realize that self-interest is not important."

"Then what is important?" I asked.

"To develop a knowledge of God's truth—His laws; how we are suppose to be living—the big picture. It's a hard thing to do, but the truths are simple, starting with a love for others."

Jack paused for a moment. "Jack, I have the sense that you have a mission for yourself," I said.

"I knew a long time ago that God was taking care of me."

"How did you know?" I asked.

"The near misses in Korea and Vietnam. At first the idea that God was looking after me was low in intensity, but then the words became visualized—crystallized. Since then that knowledge has been manifested again and again."

"Are you saying that God is saving you for something?"

"Yeah, I guess so. I know I'm just one person, but I seek to know what I'm supposed to do."

"What have you discovered?"

"I think my mission has to do with my relationships with people. I have a duty to be more aware. To pat them on their back when they need it. To give them a stroke. To show love in some fashion to my fellow man.

"I think I have the job of having a positive influence on the people I meet. Whether what I say relates to God or not doesn't matter—because it all relates to God. Whenever there is positive influence, it is God working. I think when God sees that, He is saying, 'This is how you are suppose to get along.'"

"But how do you get there?" I asked.

"When you start off in life, your view is very narrow. Then you start expanding. Over time you experience a broad array of events. Little by little your mind draws on those experiences—cataloging, digesting, filing all the information. You become more aware of what it means—then there is a revelation."

"You mean a leap in understanding?" I asked.

"Well, not exactly a leap," Jack said.

"A baby step, then?"

"How about a crawl."

We both laughed.

"The point is this," Jack continued. "The older we get, the more we see how things connect. And that makes us wiser. At first you think that *self* is everything—making money—and then you realize it's not about self; it's about what is outside of you. You become aware of those things around you: God, others, and relationships. That's what's important."

Jack's story is not uncommon. In my research, I found a positive correlation between age and spirituality. Older adults make a more conscious and persistent effort to grow spiritually than do younger adults.

However, young men and women need not grow old before choosing to look beyond their own egocentric interests. The success of the Peace Corps is a good example. Established on March 1, 1961, the Peace Corps has enlisted 155,000 volunteers. Since the Corps' inception, volunteers have served in 134 countries. The mean age of these volunteers is 28; the median age is 25. These young people are not waiting to make a difference in the lives of those who are less fortunate; they are doing it now, while they are young. These Americans (60 percent female, 40 percent male, 92 percent single) have put muscle into their spiritual lives by volunteering two years of their youth to work without pay in places like Bangladesh and Mozambique.

We adults have a responsibility to raise the awareness for our young people. Frankly, most teenagers—consumed with the market value of their own image—are insensitive to the well-being of others. To be self-centered as a teenager is quite "natural," but being "natural" is not everything. As Scott Peck once observed, pooping in our pants is *natural*—just not desirable. Some natural urges, like self-absorption, need to be harnessed. We need to take a more active role in extolling and modeling the virtues of kindness and service.

Older adults plan what they want to accomplish. Simply *going with the flow* and *doing what comes natural* suggest a breezy, laissez-faire attitude about life. Unfortunately, *going with the flow* is not a prescription for well-being. People who *plan what they want to accomplish each week* not only achieve more, but they also have a greater sense of well-being.

Going with the flow just doesn't cut it—not if you want to feel good about yourself. So, take the time to plan what you are going to accomplish for the week. Again, this is a break from doing what is *natural*. Laziness is natural; planning one's week requires discipline.

With careful planning, you are more likely to s*pend your time doing what is truly important in life.*

A COMPARISON OF WOMEN VERSUS MEN

Women are happier and more disciplined than men in the disciplines of love, service, and vision.

Women score higher on the discipline of love. Keep in mind our definition of love: The will to extend one's self for the purpose of nurturing intellectual and spiritual growth for oneself and others.

Why do women tend to be more loving than men? One theory suggests that the more testosterone, the more violent people become. Another theory is that women are more nurturing because they are socialized to be more nurturing; and men are socialized to be more aggressive.

What interests me is not why women are more loving but, rather, what can be done to encourage *men* to become more nurturing of themselves and others. According to our research, men are less passionate about learning new things; however, the most loving men bravely place themselves in the face of novelty and differences. The greatest business leaders surround themselves with a diverse staff: a cadre of men and women who are young and old, liberal and conservative, artistic and scientific. And, the strongest husbands and fathers seek to understand—and, yes, even champion—the special interests of their wives and children.

Many men become nervous when introduced to new ideas—a byproduct of male competitiveness. That is why it is refreshing when we see a leader demonstrate fidelity to diverse thinking. In the late 1930s, Alfred Sloan was chairman of the board for General Motors. On one occasion, the board received a proposal and quickly gave it their enthusiastic approval, believing the idea would yield a grand sum of money for the organization and help to crush the competition. All board members, including Alfred Sloan, voted in favor of the proposition. That was when Sloan said: "I don't like the way we are thinking about this issue. We're looking at it from one angle. I want all of you to think about it for a month and examine the idea from another perspective." One month later the idea was voted down—the board members had widened their field of vision and probably made a wiser decision.

We need more men with the courage to seek out perspectives that come from beyond their hormonal pool of puffery.

Women score higher on the discipline of service. Women score higher than men across the board when it comes to service. Women report that they are more willing to forgive and less likely to hold a grudge. Women are also less likely to get into a boxing match, less intent on proving that they are right.

Men are too often indiscriminate warriors; their battle muscles are constantly twitching, spoiling for a fight—eager to prove to anyone within earshot that they are the sole and anointed bearers of truth.

Mixing these two temperaments—female forgiveness and male aggressiveness—can create a volatile brew. It can supply the potion for a destructive, co-dependent relationship: the abusive male, the forgiving female. But it does not have to be that way, for women are also powerful visionaries: they know what they want to accomplish. If that vision is hearty enough, they will sidestep all the male posturing and pursue a higher goal. Likewise, when men exercise their responsibility muscles—particularly the ability to release the frustrating situations that are outside their control—they can counterbalance their instinct to dominate their female companions.

Women score higher on the discipline of vision. Women have greater clarity around who they want to be and what they want to accomplish.

The fact that women tend to be more clear on personal mission and objectives may stem from their disciplines of love and service. Women are inclined to be more other-centered. They are more willing to direct their energies toward nurturing and celebrating others, whereas men tend to be more egocentric—more eager to place their own interests first, to make a name for themselves. But making it big is no easy task: detours and blind alleys abound; if one venture fails, a man is likely to quickly try his hand at something else—something more promising, more tantalizing. As one man told me: "I don't know what I want to be. It depends on what I can get, and how fast I can get it."

Understanding one's direction is for many women less complicated: they love and serve—two things that can be done in any personal or professional setting. I am not suggesting that the choice of vocation is less important for a woman, or less difficult to pinpoint; I am suggesting that women appear to be more grounded during the search, more aware of the deeper purpose of any endeavor: to contribute. As a result, women tend to have a greater sense of purpose and greater peace of mind.

For example, my wife Nita has always been at peace about her career. She has always wanted to do one thing: teach children. She found her niche very early in life; she is a teacher, and she has had no other professional ambition. That certainty gave her a sense of identity and inner peace—something that I have admired through the years. In that respect, I think that Nita has fulfilled her life mission: to nurture children and to be at peace about it.

I am a different fish—representative of many other men. Throughout my life, I agonized over my career; I was continually searching for something better: something more prestigious, more creative, more lucrative. As the years rolled by, I dallied with teaching, entertaining, psychotherapy, journalism, television and radio commentating, training, consulting, and speaking—and those are just the high points. I always had itchy feet.

I suspect that men carry their ancestral hunting tendencies into the modern world—relentlessly stalking the long-toothed beast, a more majestic trophy to hang on the wall. And so we men load our weapons and trudge into the woods, cutting one new trail after the other, determined to make the ultimate kill.

Why do most women know what they want to accomplish in life, while many men wander aimlessly, squinting at the shadows on the horizon?

Ancestral programming is only part of the answer. Another, more important part, is freedom of choice. If we were to listen more to the voice of wisdom—the power within—we would be guided to a clear path to follow. Everytime I go hiking in the Cascade mountains in the Pacific Northwest, I feel realigned and revitalized. Sometimes I lose the trail, and when I do, I get out my map and compass, locate my bearings, and find my way again. Orienteering in the woods is akin to what we must do to find our way within our own lives. We must stop plodding for a moment, sit on a rock or a tree stump, examine our internal map, find a landmark on the horizon, and set a course. If we are sincere, if we seek a quiet place, if we close our eyes and ask, "What is my life's quest?" eventually, a compelling vision will emerge.

A COMPARISON OF MANAGERS VERSUS NONMANAGERS

Mangers are happier, more visionary, and more responsible than nonmanagers.

Managers are happier than nonmanagers. Are people happier because they are managers? Or are happy people promoted to management? The answer is both. Managers tend to have a greater sense of control and influence in their lives. They are involved more intimately in determining the direction of the organization. That sense of control is satisfying to the manager. On the other hand, the people who are promoted to management tend to be upbeat and hopeful: people who look at problems as challenges to be taken in stride with some old-fashioned, hard work and a joyful attitude.

Managers have greater vision than nonmanagers. This is to be expected. Managers feel more secure about who they want to be; they know what they want to accomplish; and they plan the route to get there. They are men and women who get up in the morning with a task in mind. They enjoy the feeling of being in control of their destiny, which comes—at least in part—from their internal compass.

Vision is the stock and trade of successful managers—a source of personal and interpersonal motivation. I once asked a highly respected manager to share her secret of success.

"Vision," she said. "The ability to see the finished product and, then, rally the troops to make it happen."

"What if the troops can't be rallied?" I asked.

"Then I know I haven't done my job," she said. "I haven't painted a compelling picture of the end in mind. I have to show how the project is good for everyone: the employees and the company. If I can do that, I've got a tiger by the tail."

Managers demonstrate greater responsibility than nonmanagers. Good managers don't believe in luck; they believe in elbow grease. They are not whiners, waiting for the winds of good fortune to blow their way; they make their own good fortune by diligently attacking problems.

Early in my career, I was put off by a manager who was, from my vantage point, viciously condescending. I had been tasked to interview him on a special project for the in-house newsletter. When I asked him to explain the project, I was quickly befuddled by a cascade of engineering jargon.

"Whoa, wait a minute," I said, writing furiously.

The manager narrowed his eyes. "What's the matter, sweetheart? You can't keep up? Maybe you should send someone over who can."

After the interview, I marched to my manager's office. "I will never have anything to do with that man again," I bellowed. I was trembling with anger.

My manager listened quietly. "That's a tough one," she said. "So what are you going to do about it?"

"I told you," I said, "I'm not going to work with him—ever."

"I'm afraid that's not an option, Allen. He's a vice president. You have to work with him—25 percent of the company reports to him; you can't ignore that. So what are you going to do?"

We talked for another 45 minutes. By then, we had developed a strategy: I needed to confront him and establish some communication ground rules. That was exactly what I did.

It was not easy, but after we talked through some guidelines, to my surprise, he apologized to me. In time, he became one of my favorite managers within the company.

That was a good lesson for me. My instinct was to take flight; my manager's instinct was to solve the problem—a characteristic of a responsible manager.

Managers have greater love than nonmanagers. Managers score higher than nonmanagers in helping others grow and mature. Robert Greenleaf, founder of The Center for Applied Ethics (renamed the Robert K. Greenleaf Center), taught that the most powerful leaders are servant leaders: men and women who help others to become wiser, stronger, more autonomous. The legacy is this: when an apprentice is guided by a servant leader, that apprentice eventually becomes a servant leader. Consequently, knowledge and wisdom expand exponentially.

Greenleaf noted that the enemy is not evil, stupid, or apathetic people; it is not even the system. "The enemy," he said, "is a strong, natural servant who has the potential to lead but does not lead, or who chooses to follow a nonservant."

Management is not just a privilege, it is a responsibility. To help others grow is a victory for all: the leader, the follower, the organization—everyone benefits.

World-class managers know that when it comes to building character, they have two responsibilities: first, to enhance their own discipline and, second, to encourage greater discipline in others. Naturally, that inside-out approach to character development is not limited to managers; it is the calling of all servant leaders, regardless of vocation or station in life, who desire greater joy for themselves and the people they love.

FROM THEORY TO PRACTICE: RAY'S STORY

Speaking about discipline in general, analytical terms can undercut the mystery and impact of the power within. The following story, one that is close to my heart, translates the five disciplines into specific, personal terms.

I stepped off the elevator, turned the corner, and walked to the waiting room. The family was there. They all looked pale and heavy with worry.

"How's he doing?" I asked.

My brother's wife, Jan, answered in terse sentences. "He's had a stroke, but he's okay. He has no paralysis. He can't speak."

"Where is he?"

"Down the hall," Jan said, "but he's very tired."

I knew that was Jan's way of asking me not to go in. But I was anxious to see my brother, to let him know that I was there for him. "I won't tire him," I promised. "I'll just look in for a minute."

Ray was propped up in his bed. My first rush of emotion was the grating sense of incongruence, that my brother was absurdly out of place. Polished monitors registered his vital signs in pulsing red and green lights. A nurse was preparing an IV—an anti-clotting agent, I learned later.

I walked over to the bed. "How are you doing little brother?"

Ray looked at me, smiled, and tried to say something. There was a grunt; that was all. He tried again. Still nothing. He looked at me with a mix of embarrassment and frustration. Then, without warning, he started to sob. I didn't see it coming.

"That's part of the stroke," Shelley said. I hadn't noticed that Ray's oldest daughter had followed me into the room.

Those tears broke my heart. I put my hand on my brother's shoulder. What could I do? What could I say? I wished that there were some way that I could help carry his load.

"I love you, Ray," I said. "You get some rest. Let your body heal. I'll see you tomorrow." Ray's eyes were already closing as I spoke. Then he was asleep.

The next morning I walked into Ray's room just as he was waking. I nodded to Jan and sat down on the side of the bed.

"How you doing bro?" I asked.

Ray smiled a crooked smile while hoisting himself up to a sitting position. He hunched his shoulders, his expression saying, "How am I doing? I don't have a clue; it's out of my control."

"Hey, look what I've got," I said, pulling a magnetic writing tablet from a paper sack. "It's great," I said. "If you mess up a word, just wipe the board clean and start all over again."

Ray smiled one of his big, boyish smiles.

My brother's childlike manner was a lingering characteristic of the stroke. My brother displayed a kind of innocent tenderness and vulnerability that was at once heart-warming and engaging. Everyone noticed it and was attracted to it. And they told him so.

"We like you this way," they would say.

Later in his recovery Ray talked about it.

"I don't understand," he said with tears welling up in his eyes. "Everybody says they like the way I am now. Does that mean that they didn't like me before?"

And with that Ray was sobbing uncontrollably.

"Oh, Ray," I said choking back the tears. "What they are seeing now, the gentleness, has always been there. It's part of you. It was just concealed under a thin veneer of toughness. It was always there just below the surface. You are you, Ray, and we love you—regardless of what's in the store window."

Ray took the magnetic board in hand and began to create not a word, but a drawing.

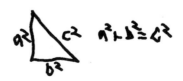

Yes, the Pythagorean theorem. "I get it," I said. "You want me to know that you can still reason. Your speech may be halted, but you can still think. Is that it?"

Ray nodded excitedly. That was a moment of connection for us. We shared a simple but wonderful discovery: Ray could still reason just fine—and that was good, that was very good.

Then, as if this insight had sucked the strength out of him, Ray's eyes began to droop. He scribbled a line on the magnetic board:

I go slep now

"Okay," I said, "I'll see you after work." Before I finished my sentence, he was sound asleep.

When I returned that evening, the family was just leaving to have dinner. I decided to stay on. I sat in a lounge chair at the side of my brother's bed, silently holding vigil. Ray was sleeping on his side, his face toward me.

When he opened his eyes and saw me there, sitting in the shadows, he began to cry. I got up from the chair and sat down on the side of his bed and made this pledge: "Ray, we will beat this thing together."

Ray smiled and clutched my hand. His grip was still firm. I remember thinking how massive and callused his fingers were—mitts accustomed to breaking down rusted bolts or wielding sticks of six-inch stainless pipe.

In a few moments, Ray had drifted off to sleep again. His grip relaxed, and I returned to the chair at the side of the bed. The minutes ticked by in the darkened room. And then I noticed that Ray's lips were moving. Was he speaking? Maybe it was possible for him to speak in his dreams—if not in his waking hours. Maybe the impulse to raise one's voice takes another route through the corridors of the brain when the body is dead to the world. Still his lips were moving.

Again, I moved to the side of his bed. His eyes were closed. I leaned over to shorten the distance between my ear and his lips.

And at that moment, Ray spoke—in the faintest of whispers—his first sentence: "I . . . just . . . w-w-want . . . to . . . t-talk."

Just five, halting, single-syllable words. And, yet, that simple sentence was a declaration of independence. It was Ray's statement of liberation. Suddenly everything was okay: Ray had a vision—the first, pivotal step to restoration.

Ray opened his eyes. He surrendered to explosive sobs that racked his body and shook the bed. I wrapped my arms around his massive shoulders. His back was dripping with sweat. I held him for a long time.

That was the beginning of Ray's recovery—the discovery of the discipline of *vision*. In the months to follow, Ray was to enlist all five disciplines.

My brother and I met every day for two hours. In the first hour, I gave Ray a speech lesson (my master's degree had been in speech).

The stroke had damaged Ray's speech center, resulting in two problems: apraxia and dysnomia. Apraxia has to do with motor planning and the diminished control and agility of tongue and lips; often, Ray knew the word he wished to articulate, but was physically unable to replicate it. Dysnomia, on the other hand, is the inability to recall words; sometimes, Ray was simply unable to connect a word with a concept.

Linguistically, Ray was on the ground floor, so we started with the basics: vowel and consonant sounds. On one of the first lessons, we worked on the "H" sound. It was nearly impossible for Ray to pronounce the word *hat*.

"Imagine that you are fogging up a mirror," I told him. "Try it."

He pursed his lips as if he were blowing out a candle. "'at," he said.

"No, *hh*hat," I repeated.

"'at."

"No. Nice try. *Hhh*hat."

Back and forth we volleyed, and each time I said *no* Ray would roll his eyes and laugh (Ray's ability to find humor in his childlike condition was a godsend in those early days). When he finally produced the semblance of an "h," I praised him profusely, and we took a break. In those first sessions, 10 minutes of focused work would wear him out.

Each day we worked on more difficult words and phrases. Progress was fast in the first few months and then, gradually, began to level off. After a year, Ray had regained between 80 to 90 percent of his speaking agility.

After a speech lesson, Ray and I would go for a walk. At first, just a couple of blocks would exhaust him. But, little by little, we increased the pace and the distance, until he was able to complete four miles in just under an hour. As the days turned into weeks, and the weeks into months, the weight started to come off. Ray, who had allowed himself to become overweight over recent years, lost 60 pounds in six months. It was not easy, but when it was done, Ray felt young again.

During this healing time, my brother became more open to expressing the discipline of *love*. One day after a speech lesson and a long walk, Ray invited me to soak with him in the hot tub on his back porch that overlooked the Columbia River. We were quiet for awhile, watching the Canadian geese sail overhead toward the river's edge. It was a good day. Ray felt good about the progress he was making with his speech. And I felt closer to him than ever before. There was something about the stroke that broke through Ray's wall of stoicism and control. He was usually very guarded about his expression of affection. That changed. He told me he loved me more in the first five days following his stroke than in the previous five years.

I felt so close to my brother at that moment, I decided to ask him about our "dark ages"—the 10 years as young adults when we hardly spoke to each other.

"Those years were very sad for me," I said. "I just never felt accepted by you."

"It wasn't that I didn't accept you," Ray said. "It was that I couldn't accept myself. I was not where I needed to be. I was so unsure about myself, I couldn't tolerate differences."

THE RESULTS

"I'm not sure I understand," I said.

"There was a war raging inside me. I wanted to do right and, yet, I repeatedly failed. I turned the frustration of my own shortcomings on you." Ray was speaking softly and with absolute certainty.

I grabbed his hand and squeezed; he covered my hand with his own. "I understand, now," I said. "Thanks, Ray."

"I love you, Al."

My brother began to speak of *responsibility*. One day, I drove Ray to an appointment with his occupational therapist. My brother started speaking about changes he wanted to make in his life.

"It sounds like you are serious about taking care of yourself," I noted.

"Yes," he said solemnly. "I was not responsible to my loved ones. Really, I was playing Russian roulette with them—putting in 16-hour days and getting heavier all the time. I don't know how I got out of control, but it is in my power to be responsible again. And I will." Tears were streaming down his cheeks.

My mind was scrambling. Ray's call for responsibility was momentous; I wanted to somehow accent the importance of his words. And so I said, "That's good, Ray. *Really* good." My brother could never know the depth of meaning I placed on those words.

Then, there were signs of *commitment*. After a 30-minute speech lesson one day, Ray got uncharacteristically philosophical. "People think I'm a hero," he started. "I'm no hero, I just survived. I abused my body. That's not heroism. Now is the time to be heroic—when I'm ashamed or tired or depressed, when I don't feel like exercising or eating right—now is the time to buck up and take care of myself."

"I hope it becomes a way of life for the rest of your life," I said, "not just a diet or an exercise program that you discard after two or three weeks."

"It has to be," Ray said, "or it will be a very short life."

And there were indications of *service*. Three months after his stroke, Ray was already thinking about serving other people.

"I have been thinking about Uncle John," Ray said one day, referring to Mom's 80-year-old, Greek brother, a venerable master at loving people. "He's getting along in years. I think it's important that I see him, that I spend some time with family."

A few weeks later my brother and I flew to Denver to visit Uncle John and Aunt Soitera.

We sat in John's modest living room and listened to him tell familiar stories about the war in Italy. Ray listened intently and said, "I love you, Uncle John." I watched as Ray leaned over the family patriarch and kissed him on the cheek.

Uncle John patted Ray on his back with his strong, gnarled hands and said, "You're a good boy, Sonny."

Six years have come and gone since Ray's stroke, and the story is not yet finished. It will never be finished. Everyday, Ray applies the discipline required to stand and deliver. It has not always been easy (often a stroke survivor gets worse before he gets better). But in the face of daunting and humbling trials—some that have seemingly assaulted him with random vengeance—my brother has taken the heat and emerged, like tempered steel, stronger for having survived the test of fire.

A stroke leaves a man in a different state of mind. Some of the changes are perplexing and difficult to reconcile—a penalty that transforms even modest endeavors into feats of heroic proportions. Today, I find that my brother has become, by necessity, amazingly diligent—doing whatever he must to make things work out—and increasingly wise (he no longer sweats the small stuff). Does he have farther to travel? Sure, as do we all. I love him so much; I think I'll ask him if I can tag along.

Part II:

FIVE DISCIPLINES OF EFFECTIVENESS

In this section, we will explore each of the five disciplines in depth.

Chapter 5, "The Discipline of Love: The Path of Mind and Soul," defines love as "the will to extend ourselves for the purpose of intellectual and spiritual development for oneself and others." I explore the ramifications of that definition and introduce the four irreducible components of love: to learn, to be free, to teach, and to serve. This chapter offers a fresh and rich approach to satisfying what is easily our greatest human need: the need to love and be loved.

Chapter 6, "The Discipline of Responsibility: The Path of Choice," advances the power of making principle-centered decisions, regardless of the situation—a capacity made possible through the application of higher-order competencies. I explain that we are driven by needs and that those needs can be satisfied in a way that is both honorable and life sustaining. This chapter provides a whole new understanding of what it means to be internally motivated.

Chapter 7, "The Discipline of Vision: The Path of Nobility and Revolution," is, like the *Declaration of Independence*, a call for nobility (life, liberty, and pursuit of happiness) and revolution (freedom by the people, for the people). This chapter pays tribute to brave intentions and transformational behaviors. I present a wide range of examples—from historical saints and heroes to ordinary people with extraordinary visions. Finally, I introduce you to a compelling rationale and straightforward strategy for creating your own declaration of independence.

Chapter 8, "The Discipline of Commitment: The Path of Truth and Importance," is about dissolving prejudices. It praises earnest and open-minded seekers of truth—the insatiable learners who readily admit their relative ignorance. It also celebrates the people who attend to important relationships with family, friends, intimates, and co-workers—always striving to create alliances that are fully trusting and joyful. The chapter ends with a strategy for slaying one of the greatest enemies of effectiveness—procrastination.

Chapter 9, "The Discipline of Service: The Path of Mercy and Grace," begins by extolling the virtue of forgiveness—even when the other's behavior is reprehensible. Building on that foundation, I offer four ways to make the spirit of service come alive: through the formation of community, the art of listening, the resolution of conflict, and the simple acts of kindness.

Chapter 5

THE DISCIPLINE OF LOVE

THE PATH OF MIND AND SOUL

The most fundamental kind of love, which underlies all types of love, is brotherly love. By this I mean the sense of responsibility, care, respect, knowledge of any other human being, the wish to further his life.

—Eric Hoffer

Jack Cloud is from Montana. He grew up with a fly rod in one hand and a 32-caliber Winchester in the other. He is a man's man. That means he doesn't send Valentine cards, never eats anything he can't pronounce, and always wears pointed-toe, lizard skin, cowboy boots—even to church, which he only frequents when someone in the family is "hatched, matched, or dispatched." He's the kind of guy who won't stand any closer than 45 inches to another man—the exact length of a Browning over-and-under, 12-gauge shotgun. It's not that he's mean; he's just careful about anything quiche-like.

Jack once attended a workshop I conducted on communication in the workplace. I don't know why he chose to come; maybe he misread the title and expected ammunition in the workplace—I'm not sure. In any case, he was there, and I treated him like I treat everyone else, with care and tenderness—all that gooey stuff that makes a guy like Jack want to puke.

At one point in the workshop, we began to talk about crediting others. That led to a discussion on the practice of telling family members we love them.

"I don't do that," Jack said. "My grandpa never did, and my dad never did—but I knew they loved me. They told me every day."

"How did they do that?" I asked.

"They gave me noogies." Jack demonstrated by wrapping his left arm around the neck of an imaginary loved one and rubbing the knuckles of his right hand across the scalp of the phantom victim.

"I can see how noogies might be very expressive," I said. Still, I wondered if a noogie were a legitimate substitute for the actual words. I decided to challenge him. "Jack, do you have any children?"

"Sure do," he said. "Taylor, my two-year-old daughter."

"Is she important to you?"

"More than you'll ever know," he said immediately.

"Do you tell her you love her?" I asked.

"Yep, everyday. But I'm also phasing in noogies."

"How about your wife? Do you tell her you love her?"

"No. It's different with my wife. I tell her in other ways."

"How's that?"

"I tell her every time I mow the lawn. With every swath I take, the motor rumbles, 'I love you, I love you, I love you . . . .'" Jack was smiling when he said this; still, we knew there was a great deal of truth in his words.

The group enjoyed Jack's expression of love but wondered if Jack's wife was missing something by not hearing the words. A lively debate ensued.

After about 20 minutes of discussion, Jack finally broke down. "Okay, okay, you've got me," he said. "Tonight, I'm mowing the lawn. I'll cut the words 'I love you' into the grass—right there in front of God and everyone. How much can it hurt; it'll grow out in three days."

The group laughed, and we moved on to a new subject.

Toward the end of the workshop, we began to summarize the key principles of effective communication. After everyone else had contributed, Jack looked me straight in the eyes—his cue that he was ready.

"Jack? You have something?"

"For me," he said, "I always want to live a life of absolute integrity."

"What does that mean?" I asked.

"Well, this may not make sense to you," Jack said, "but, for me, it means living like Roy Rogers."

For the next 10 minutes, Jack waxed eloquently on the virtues of the Singing Cowboy. Before we knew it, the idea hit us like a wild horse stampede. What a concept. The more we thought about it, the more sense it made. And why not; he was the ultimate buckaroo of discipline.

Roy Rogers was *responsible*. You could always rely on him to make good choices. He was a man of his word, fully trustworthy. If Roy said he would do it, you could take it to the bank—no exceptions, no disappointments. His choices were not only as true as leather, but gentle to boot—even a little sentimental. He could sing a love song to a ring of trail-weary cowpokes and punctuate it with a kiss on the lips of his horse, Trigger.

Roy was a *visionary*, dedicated to noble pursuits. He always fought for justice and fair play. He was virtuous; he did the right thing. He never used a fence post on a bad guy, never kicked a man when he was down. He did what had to be done—in the mildest way possible—to bring the desperados to justice.

Roy was *committed* to truth. On that he stood his ground. He was willing to face incredible odds—half-a-dozen, burly bandits with black hats, punched-in faces, and disagreeable tempera-ments—and somehow walk away with his hat unsmudged and his teeth unshuffled. And when it came to loyalty, they don't make 'em any more committed. Roy never turned his back on a friend in need. He never put his horse to bed wet. He never circled up the boys in the bunkhouse and talked low-down and no-good about Dale Evans—or anything else pure and holy.

Roy was a man devoted to *service*. Again and again, he stood up for the down-trodden: women in distress, children in danger, homesteaders under the rule of malicious landlords or villainous gunslingers.

And, Roy Rogers always said "*I love you*" without saying a word: a wink, a slap on the back, and, maybe, a couple of noogies for Gabby.

Isn't that it? The real code of the West: responsibility, vision, commitment, service, and love? What a mission statement: the doctrine according to Roy Rogers. No wonder the Singing Cowboy had so many happy endings; how could he lose with a foundation that disciplined, a purpose that noble?

By the way, Jack did not stick around at the end of the workshop. He didn't shake my hand or say goodbye. But in the closing moments of the last session, he made this speech: "Thanks, Allen. That was one helluva Powder River ride, cowboy."

●　　●　　●

WHOLE-HEART LIVING

My mother was raised in an orphanage in Brooklyn, New York during the great depression. She tells me that when she was a schoolgirl, she always walked with her head down, eyes darting, hoping to find a few pennies, a nickel, or a dime. And when she did, it was an occasion for celebration (in the early 1930's 10 cents could get you into the movies).

Years later, when I was a small boy, my mother routinely did something that puzzled me. After making a purchase at a store downtown, she would walk into the sunlight, uncurl her hand, and let the change from her recent transaction tumble to the pavement. I was not, under any circumstances, allowed to retrieve the coins.

"But, why not?" I pleaded.

"Because those pennies belong to a poor little girl less fortunate than you," she would say. "It will make her day."

I didn't know it then, but my mother was teaching me the whole-heart approach to living—the ultimate path to mind and soul. What is whole-heart living? To answer that question, we must revisit an introductory lesson on the anatomy of the human heart.

The heart has four chambers. The upper chambers are called the left and right auricles. The lower chambers are called the left and right ventricles. The two auricle chambers draw the blood from the veins. When the blood pressure builds in the auricles, the tricuspid and mitral valves open, and the blood pours into the lower ventricle chambers. When the ventricle chambers fill, the pulmonary and aortic valves open, the heart contracts, and the blood is pushed through the arteries to the rest of the body. This two-step process—diastole and systole—occurs every second of our lives.

I use this anatomical wonder as a metaphor for personal development. Earlier I drew on Scott Peck's definition of love as *the will to extend one's self for the purpose of nurturing intellectual or spiritual growth for oneself and others*. I believe that definition captures the essence of a successful life—a process that resembles the beating of the human heart.

Imagine that the heart did not beat every second, but only once in a lifetime with diastole occurring at birth and systole following about 40 years later. In the first half of that single heartbeat—the first half of our lives—the heart relaxes, and the blood is drawn into the two auricle chambers.

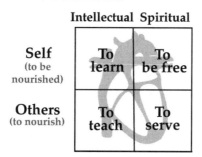

	Intellectual	Spiritual
Self (to be nourished)	To learn	To be free
Others (to nourish)	To teach	To serve

The function of the auricles is akin to the nourishing of the intellectual and spiritual self. The auricle chambers (self) must first be nourished before nourishing the ventricle chambers (others). This is first-half living, with emphasis upon serving one's self—a period when young people seek to make a name for themselves.

In the second half of the human heartbeat, the ventricle chambers fill up, the heart contracts, and blood is pushed out of the heart and into the body. The functioning of the ventricle chambers is analogous to nourishing the intellect and spirit of others. This is second-half living. Now the shift has been made from climbing the ladder of success to making a contribution to the community.

Unfortunately, for many people that transition—from receiving blood to giving blood, from being nourished to nourishing—is arrested. These people get stuck in the diastolic phase of their lives (self-centeredness), frantically marketing their gifts for the world to adore, somehow unwilling or incapable of making the transition to the systolic phase of their lives (other-centeredness). When systole does not occur, the heart has fulfilled only half its mission. Obviously, half a heartbeat is fatal; similarly, half a life lived is, if not fatal, certainly tragic.

In summary, during diastole the healthy heart relaxes and receives the blood; during systole it contracts and delivers the blood. Likewise, a healthy life must be distinguished by first receiving nourishment and then delivering it.

TO BE NOURISHED

There are two chambers of the heart dedicated to serving the individual: the intellectual (to learn) and the spiritual (to be free). Both chambers must function flawlessly to ensure personal success.

Nourishing the Intellect of Self: To Learn

Successful people are learners. They have a hardy curiosity for all things. They want to understand the world they live in. They constantly seek ways to expand the depth and breadth of their knowledge.

Learners are builders of knowledge. These learners understand the cumulative nature of education. Earl Nightingale, the famous motivational speaker, once said that if people were to read for one hour every day within their discipline, by the end of three years they would be at the top of their fields. At the end of five years, they would be national experts. At the end of seven years, they would be international experts. I do not doubt this prediction.

Learners are system thinkers. The more we read, the more we see the interconnectedness of things. In-depth system thinking is what separates the master of any discipline from the apprentice. Consider the most extraordinary classical composers—Bach, Mozart, Beethoven, Brahms. These musical geniuses understood the interconnectedness of every note on the page, every nuance of tempo, dynamics, and timbre. They knew every orchestral instrument inside out—the range and tonal quality of strings, brass, woodwinds, and percussion alike. Of course, they were experts. Why? Because they understood the total musical system.

Very few of us are musical geniuses. But we do have the capacity to become system thinkers within our own discipline. The electrician who not only knows how to string cable, but also understands the theory and application of electricity, is a system thinker. The manager who enhances his or her understanding of project management with the art of human relations is a system thinker. The gardener who supplements knowledge of seeds and seedlings with soil, fertilizer, pruning, and irrigation is a system thinker.

Learners are readers. But system thinking is more the exception than the rule—at least if the volume of reading among Americans is any indication. The figures are dismal. On the average, Americans read less than one book a year. In fact, it has been said that 58 percent of all high school graduates will never read another nonfiction book cover to cover. This trend is deeply disturbing.

One day, I spoke to an animated 17-year-old boy.

"What are you passionate about?" I asked (one of my favorite questions).

"Horses," he said. "I love everything about horses."

"Wow," I said, "if that's the case, you've got to read *The Man Who Listens to Horses* by Monty Roberts. It's terrific."

The young man smiled sheepishly. "Oh, I don't read, dude," he said flatly.

"What do you mean?" I asked.

"Oh, I like books with lots of pictures. You know, comic books—stuff like that."

It was not that the young man *couldn't* read ("He's quite bright," his father told me later), but that he *wouldn't* read. I wondered if this young man would grow into an old man's body with a teenager's mind.

Learners are experiencers. Reading is a marvelous resource that allows even the most timid to enter the world of incredible thinkers, but it is not the only way to learn. Learning from experience can be equally powerful. But for the most elegant learners, the simple act of having an experience is not enough. They realize that to have the same experience again and again without insight (or different experiences with the same insight) is not learning. In fact, "Insanity is doing the same thing over and over and expecting different results."

Learning through experience requires a discerning mind. Have you ever wondered how some people can go through marriages as if they were disposable commodities? Why is that? Was nothing learned the first or second or *n*th time around? The answer, unhappily, may be *no*. Learning from experience only occurs when the mind is aware, and when that fresh awareness germinates new, more effective behavior.

The first year my wife and I were married, 32 years ago, I began using the phrase, *don't be a dummy*, on my new bride. Although I meant nothing by it, the harm was done.

"You hurt my feelings when you say that to me," my wife finally confessed.

"But I don't mean anything by it," I protested.

"It doesn't matter," she said with her brown eyes shining. "It still hurts."

How could I not be moved? "Honey, I won't say it again. I promise."

I have kept that promise for over three decades and will continue to keep it as long as I live. I learned from that little experience. I became aware of how words can cut—even when offered in innocence. If I had not been aware, if I had continued to violate my wife in that way, it could have easily damaged the marriage.

To ignore that learning, coupled with a few learnings more, could rock, even shatter, a marriage.

Nourishing the Spirit of Self: To Be Free.

What does it mean to be free? I posed that question to a teenager recently. His response: "Freedom is doing whatever you want, whenever you want to do it."

But is *that* freedom? Hardly. I'd say it's more like defiance, and defiance is a form of dependency, the opposite of freedom: "I'll prove to you that I'm not under your thumb; I'll do whatever I damn well please." Defiance is fiercely competitive and cannot be played without the presence of another player—creating a debilitating dance of dependency.

So what is freedom? I'll answer that question by beginning with what it is not.

Freedom is not game playing. Defiance is not the only kind of dependency that people resort to. Some take on the role of victim. Others take on the role of rescuer. Still others like to play the persecutor (Karpman, 1972). These little dramas are played out everyday in homes and offices. Here is an office example.

Situation: A young, overzealous, internal auditor is berating Kim, a shy and insecure file clerk. The manager, Frank, is Kim's supervisor, a guy who tends to "shoot from the hip."

Auditor: *[As persecutor]* I find your filing system incredibly disorganized. Folders are missing; labels are gone. It takes hours to retrieve the simplest information. This is absolutely unacceptable!

Clerk: *[As victim]* I'm sorry. There is just so much to do around here. I know it's important, but I just feel like I'm going crazy sometimes. You can't believe the headache I've got.

Manager: *[As persecutor and rescuer]* What is going on here? *[To auditor]* Where do you get off talking to my people

	in that tone of voice? *[To clerk]* Kim, you don't have to stand for that kind of abuse.
Clerk:	*[As rescuer]* Well, he really was only doing his job. I'm sure that auditing is a very difficult assignment.
Auditor:	*[As victim]* Hey, forget it. I don't need this aggravation. I was only trying to keep you out of trouble. See what you get for trying to help out. A slap in the face. *[Exits]*
Clerk:	*[As persecutor]* Frank, I'm surprised at how you treated that young man. It's obvious he's new at the job, and you berated him.
Manager:	*[Victim]* What? I can't believe you just said that. I was just looking out for your best interests—you know, taking care of my people and all. But that's okay. If you don't need my help, who am I to argue?
Clerk:	*[As rescuer]* Oh, Frank.

Does any of this sound familiar? It's a popular game. Although some players stick with a single role—persecutor, victim, or rescuer—for a lifetime, often the roles are switched at a moment's notice, allowing the player to take greater advantage of the situation. The point of the game is to set the other players in the game off balance to get what you want: a sense of self-importance, sympathy, or the upper hand.

Freedom is not arrogance. Freedom must never be confused with arrogance. Arrogance is a manifestation of the ego—expressed through a compulsive urge to be right—and, as such, is just another form of dependency. Why? Arrogance does not flower in solitude; it only emerges within a community of souls who are, in the mind of the arrogant, less brilliant, less accomplished, less powerful. The arrogant must have their own court: a submissive or, at least, unwitting audience to provide contrast to their egocentric "splendor."

Freedom, on the other hand, is never haughty; it is neutral. Those who are free do not berate or demean others; there is no need, for they are founded on something much more stable than the variance and unpredictability of human behavior; they are founded on principles. If one abides by principles, especially grace and mercy (the subject of Chapter 9), arrogance cannot survive—it is incompatible with laws of the spirit.

I'm still working at removing arrogance from my behavioral repertoire. In fact, arrogance almost got me drummed out of graduate school. One of my professors, a venerable, white-haired scholar, matched my arrogance step for step. He had the annoying habit of dismissing a student's point with the flick of his hand. I got the distinct impression that he did not relish thinkers, but a chorus of acolytes—tough going for me.

One day I could not contain myself. It happened during a class session on group therapy. The professor was, to my mind, plodding along at a glacial pace. I found myself filling in all the "o's" in my notes. Then he said something that made me look up from my doodling: "In group therapy you must forbid your clients from interacting outside the counseling sessions."

"I disagree," I said without thinking. My classmates were startled. "In fact," I continued, "I think Carl Rogers would support my position." Then I explained why.

I thought that quoting Carl Rogers was a nice touch. He was one of America's most respected psychologists—clearly an authority on the subject.

The professor clucked his tongue, clearly irritated by the interruption. By then, the room temperature had jumped one or two seasons. My fellow students were nervous, and so I let it go—for the time being.

But that evening I began replaying in my mind what had happened. I was still absolutely sure that Dr. Rogers would have agreed with me. So I did something outrageous: I set up a tape recorder and telephoned the famous psychologist at his home in California. I couldn't believe it when he actually answered the phone; I immediately recognized his voice from his instructional videotapes on counseling.

I told him how much I admired his work and then asked him to comment on the issue I had raised in class.

He agreed with me! And I had it all on tape to prove it.

The next day in class, I took a hot-blooded, death-defying plunge into an ocean of arrogance. As my professor started his lecture, I raised my hand. "Excuse me, sir," I said. "You remember the conversation we had yesterday regarding the formation of outside relationships among group therapy members."

"Of course," the professor said, his words laced with suspicion and impending doom. "I thought we had laid that to rest?"

"Well, not quite, sir," I said, ignoring all signals for caution. "This is what Carl Rogers has to say about it." Time seemed to slip into slow motion as I pressed the *play* button on the portable tape machine.

The professor said nothing. He just stared at me with a closed, menacing half smile. I did not like that look. Two days later, the department head told me I was on probation for my act of arrogance. In that instant, I saw nearly three years of work fall into the wastebasket. It took a lot of backpedaling (including a contrite apology to every member of the department), but, incredibly, I was able to repair the damage and salvage my degree.

In those days my ego, with its manic fixation to be right, took on gargantuan proportions. I saw life as an enormous game of one-upmanship. That is arrogance in all its glory. Forget that the professor engaged in the same game—his flick of the hand, his ominous silence—that was his choice. In those days I was just beginning to learn that I, too, had a choice: to live a life of dependency, one characterized by challenging others and flaunting my ego and intellect, or a life of freedom, characterized by kindness and a willingness to do the right thing despite outside influences.

Freedom is not anger. People who shake their fists in the air and shout, "Power to us," are also living lives of dependency. They are immersed in game playing. They once played the role of victim. Now they are playing the role of persecutor. Although the role they have selected for themselves is different, the game is still one of dependency.

You often see special interest groups engage in this kind of chest thumping: we're important, we're powerful, and you need to respect us. These tirades are, more often than not, delivered in anger, the explosive release of pent-up resentment. Do not misunderstand me. I am not suggesting that injustices should be ignored; I am suggesting that injustices should be handled with thoughtful and principled deliberation—for real freedom occurs when one defends truth with a spirit of kindness; anything less is dependency.

I remember watching the NCAA college basketball finals one year. It was a hard-fought battle between the first- and second-ranked basketball teams in the country. Almost everyone predicted that the first-ranked team would win. It was a hard-fought game of grace and strength on both sides, but in the end the underdog team emerged victorious.

At the last buzzer all spectators witnessed the inevitable agony of defeat and ecstasy of victory, but there was something else, something that disturbed me—a feeling of celebration, yes, but also a feeling of anger, even rage. One victor, a gifted shooting guard, ran to the on-floor television camera with hands clenched and shouted, "We shook the world, we shook the world." At the same time, another star teammate stalked across the court with his chest puffed-up, his teeth bared, and his eyes piercing with fire.

Much of that can be written off as youthful exuberance and bravado, but some of it is an expression of unbridled anger: "We were not respected, and now we are—and you need to give us our proper due."

Let me offer a contrasting example. I have always been impressed with the coaching strategy of the legendary, UCLA basketball coach, John Wooden. His assistant coach for four years (and later Brigham Young University's head coach for eight years), Frank Arnold, once summarized Wooden's philosophy. "He never used the words 'win' or 'beat,'" Arnold explained. "He simply said to his players: 'Go out there and play so that when the game is over, and you return to the locker room, you can look yourself in the mirror and know that you did your very best. If you are able to do that, I also think you will be happy with the outcome of the score.'" Arnold said that Wooden rarely looked at film of opposing teams; rather, he drilled his own teams on basketball fundamentals.

Do you see the difference? Wooden taught his players to be internally driven. That introspective strategy removes angry competition from the picture. Games of dependency dissolve—even for basketball players—when the only competition is the player in the looking glass.

Freedom is independence. So, if freedom is not game playing, arrogance, or anger, what is it? The essence of freedom is independence. And independence means standing on the rock of principles, doing the right thing regardless of the games others choose to play. Those who are truly independent make decisions based on their highest ideals, despite other influences.

Those who are mature enough to understand the true meaning of independence do not live lives of dependency. They do not engage in game playing. They do not whine about their misfortune; they do not look for ways to undermine others; they do not wait helplessly to be rescued from their misery. They are their own masters—a way of being that is so attractive that it spawns a cadre of followers and supporters.

For example, one day a manager summoned me to his office. "What's the status of the X9000 project?" he barked.

"I don't know," I said.

The manager's face turned crimson. "Well, Johnson, don't you think you damn well *should* know!"

Obviously, the manager was intent on playing the role of a persecutor, and likely wanted me to play the role of a victim—not the kind of game that promotes freedom. I decided not to pick up the gauntlet.

"Frankly," I said, "I have not been involved in the project. Kirk has been heading that up. However, if you would like to use me, I'd be glad to oblige." I had to compose the next sentence carefully. If the tone was not right, I could sound like a persecutor, and the dependency game would be revived. "By the way," I said, in a calm voice, "it's very important to me that we speak to each other adult to adult. I wasn't totally satisfied with the quality of our last exchange. What do you think?"

Thank goodness, the manager had the maturity to reevaluate his behavior. "Allen, you're right," he said. "Let's start this conversation over."

You don't have to be sucked into the game; you can spin out of the escalating spiral of dependency and simply level with the other person—openly and without condescension or condemnation.

TO NOURISH

For mature individuals, the second halves of their lives are truly the glory years. All the oxygenated blood that they drew into their heart is now pumped into the body. It is time to give back—serving the intellect and spirit of others through teaching and leaving a legacy. It is the gift of love.

Nourishing the Intellect of Others: To Teach

Mature, second-half people are world-class reference librarians. They rejoice in sharing what they know with others; in fact, it is one of their greatest pleasures. They abhor the pettiness of hoarding information—the ultimate loss to humanity.

Second-half people recognize that teaching benefits both the teacher and the student. The teacher cements his or her knowledge through teaching. The student captures that knowledge and applies it to his or her world of experience. Finally, the student becomes the teacher. As a result, knowledge spirals and communal knowledge increases

Gifted teachers take their time in establishing the playing field. They understand that two things must happen before they teach: they must model integrity, and they must listen.

Teachers model integrity. The consummate teachers demonstrate their wisdom by matching their behavior to their principles. The secretary to Mahatma Gandhi was once asked how the legendary leader could make a two-hour speech without a single note. His response was telling. "You do not understand. Gandhi is all one: What he feels is what he thinks; what he thinks is what he says; what he says is what he does." The great teachers are like that; they are whole. As Gandhi once said, "One cannot do right in one department of life whilst he is occupied in doing wrong in any other department. Life is one indivisible whole."

The best teachers model such wholeness. Their lives are text books of integrity, for they know that one noble act speaks louder than 10,000 words. St. Francis of Assisi once said: "Preach the gospel at all times; if necessary, use words."

Teachers are phenomenal listeners. Superior teachers listen with a rare intensity. They listen patiently and wholeheartedly. They listen for both content and emotion—and make certain that their understanding matches the intention of the speaker. Rushing an emotional speaker into problem-solving can be deadly; that's a lesson that I learned the hard way. Once, during a team-building session, I asked the participants if they felt that they were suited for the positions they held. One of the members caught me off guard.

"I'm too stupid to do my job," she said with a trembling voice.

Wanting to bolster her self-esteem, I said, "Do you really expect me to believe that?"

At that point, the woman gathered her materials and left the room. I followed her to the parking lot and tried to persuade her to return. She would not budge.

"How can I?" she said. "I can't trust you. I told you how I felt and you pounced on me. It was like calling me a liar."

She was right. Although my intention was honorable, my method was deadly. I was too anxious to teach and not patient enough to listen. Truly elegant teachers spend 90 percent of their time listening, 10 percent of their time teaching. There is a reason for that: All the time the teacher is listening, the "student" is working out his or her own problems—a great use of time.

Teachers are skilled technicians. The best teachers are sensational at making the links—at moving a student from attention to concept to demonstration to application (McCarthy, 1987).

• *Gain attention.* Skilled teachers are masters at piquing the curiosity of their students—often by creating a visceral experience. They are enormously inventive in capturing the imagination of their students. When I taught high school English, I began a lesson on Edgar Allan Poe by having the students sit in a circle on the floor of the auditorium stage and then reading *The Raven* by candlelight in my spookiest Vincent Price voice. Some may have thought I was a little goofy, but I did have my students' attention.

• *Present the concept.* Lecturing is only one way to present a concept. It is also the most lethal. A dry lecture can sap the curiosity of even the most willing students. There are scores of other alternatives: dramatic enactments, role plays, debates, story telling, analogies, question and answer, experiments, and impromptu symposiums, among others. Ideas can be presented in a myriad of ways—approaches that stimulate not only the sense of hearing, but one or more of the other senses.

• *Demonstrate the concept.* Talking about an idea is not enough; master teachers demonstrate the concept. If it's an art lesson, they get their hands in the paint; if it's a speech lesson, they deliver an oration; if it's a business lesson, they create the ledger. Then they invite their students to follow suit, to experience the new skill, to get it into their blood. This stage is fun—the magic of seeing the world in a new way.

• *Apply the concept.* Teaching is not complete until the students can apply the new concept to their lives. At this stage they transfer the learning to their own experiences. They may modify the ideas to suit their own needs. And, as evidence of their learning, they teach the new concept in an expanded version to *their* students.

Examples of poor and good teaching. In the summer between my sophomore and junior year in college, I landed a job at the local paper mill. The morning of the first day, I loaded broken-down cardboard boxes onto wooden pallets. The load was hauled away by a forklift and stacked on the other side of the warehouse. After a couple of hours my hands were red and swollen from tiny paper cuts.

After lunch the foreman, a swarthy middle-aged man, tapped me on the shoulder. "Johnson, follow me," he said in a loud voice.

I followed the foreman to the print shop. "You see that press," the foreman said. I looked at the giant waffle iron with raised, one-inch letters laid out in mirror image across the cast-iron surface.

"Yes, sir," I sang out.

"See this bucket?" the foreman asked. He pointed to a coffee can full of a smoke-gray solvent the consistency of motor oil. Then he tilted his head in the general direction of the giant waffle-iron. "Make it shine," he instructed.

I loved my new job. I wanted to be the best letter cleaner in the plant. Draped over the edge of the can was a limp rag. I picked it up and twisted one corner like I was preparing to clean out my ears and dipped the tip of the rag into the solvent. I wiped the excess off on the lip of the bucket. Then I worked the nubbin of cloth around each crevice of each character on the press. Forty-five minutes later I had finished six letters. I stepped back to admire my work.

Just then the foreman returned. "Hey, Johnson, what the deuce are you doin'?" he shouted. He didn't seem happy.

"Well, I . . . I'm cleaning the press," I stammered.

"You college know-it-all's," he muttered. "Gimme that rag." The foreman dunked rag and fist into the can of solvent. The gooey stuff sloshed over the side of the can and onto the concrete floor. He swashed the rag across the press. Solvent, sweat, and spit splattered all over. It was awesome: in three strokes the entire press was glistening. He turned, looked at me with disgust, and issued a single, sardonic guffaw. Three days later I was fired.

That foreman knew a lot about cleaning presses, but he didn't know a thing about teaching people. Although he had my attention, he took no time to present the concept, demonstrate the process, or oversee the application.

Years later—long after my short stint at the paper mill—I was teaching at a community college in Pendleton, Oregon. Murray Innes was one of the first people I met; we became friends almost immediately. I was intrigued by his devotion to the fine arts. He loved Shakespeare, the romantic poets, and classical music, particularly Brahms. His interest in music captivated me.

I had always been drawn to classical music but had little understanding of it. I knew nothing about the periods, the structure of compositions, and even less about the composers. But I wanted to learn.

One day I asked Murray if he would share his knowledge of classical music with me. Right away I knew that I had struck a chord. His eyes widened with delight. "I would like that very much, " he said.

We agreed to meet at his home once a week. Murray's agenda was precise. He would start by playing an example from the period that we were studying. "Listen to this," he'd say with a gleam in his eye, and then he would crank up the volume on, say, Mussorgsky's *Night on Bald Mountain*.

Then Murray and I would discuss the times of that particular period of music—the political, social, and literary influences. Next, Murray would reveal the structure of symphonies or concertos or sonatas—punctuating his point with recordings from his enormous library of music.

Then Murray would say, "It's time to play 'Name that Tune.'" He would drop the needle on a disc and after a moment turn to me. "What period does this come from?" he would ask. "Is it a symphony or a concerto? Who was the composer?" Sometimes I got it right, but it didn't matter (not to Murray, nor to me); I was learning, and it was wonderful.

At the end of each session, Murray would pull out records from six to 10 composers from the period. "Oh, you've got to hear this, " he would say, "and this one is an absolute must—you'll love it." I always left with a stack of albums tucked under my chin.

That was teaching. Murray was a master at gaining my attention, presenting the concept, demonstrating the concept, and helping me to apply and incorporate the music into my being. Now, years later, I am able to speak of any period of classical music with confidence, but, more, a sensitivity to and appreciation for musical ideas and emotions. The music is a part of me. I credit Murray's teaching for that personal transformation.

To this day, whenever I listen to the power of a Mahler symphony or the gentleness of a Chopin nocturne, I think to myself, "Thank you, Murray; you were the best." Whenever I think about the foreman at the paper mill, I think of something else.

Nourishing the Spirit of Others: To Serve

The most evolved leaders—those who are firmly standing in the second half of their lives—are intent on living lives of significance. As leaders of substance, they have both the honor and the responsibility to be a positive influence. Moreover, they know that leadership is best realized through service, which—to cite Mother Teresa again—is the fruit of love and the path to personal peace.

These people are the givers; they hold nothing back. They have no time for pettiness—one-upmanship, backbiting, turf building, and political infighting—only time to make a contribution.

Service is the gateway to peace. When the calling to contribute is ignored, peace becomes maddeningly illusive. I have a friend (I'll call him Andy) who, financially, was very successful early in life. He had made a small fortune in marketing by the time he was 40. At 45, he decided to retire and dedicate his life to fly fishing in the Pacific Northwest. Ten years later, he was suffering from anxiety attacks, damaged relationships, and intense boredom.

One afternoon he called me from his log house in Montana. "What should I do?" he asked. "I'm bored out of my mind."

I said, "Andy, you'll never be happy until you discover a way to make a contribution."

"How do I do that?"

"Well, think about the things you are passionate about and then share that passion with others. For example, you're an expert fly fisherman, so, how about starting a fly fishing course for kids?"

"Nah, I would never do that."

"Well, you love the Civil War. How about starting a Civil War discussion group?"

"No, I don't think so."

"Okay, I know you're crazy about collecting coins. How about teaching a community class on the subject?"

"What, and have people learn what I've got, so they can rob me blind?"

I gave up. To this day, Andy remains isolated, self-absorbed, and, ultimately, disillusioned. Those feelings will not change until he enters the second half of his life.

Service is the antithesis of ego. Leaders who have embraced a life of service never seek to prove they are right and that others are wrong; such behavior is completely alien to them. They are driven by spirit, not by ego. In his book, *Your Sacred Heart*, Wayne Dyer writes: "If you have a choice between being right or being kind, choose being kind."

For example, imagine entering a department store. Just as you are about to step through the door, you notice a woman who appears to be in a hurry. Out of courtesy, you hold the door open for her. She passes through without saying thank you. If you call out to the woman, "You're welcome," you are operating from the ego. It is saying, "Let me take a moment out of my day to make you a better person. You are not operating by my standards, and you need to be fixed."

Again, people who are living securely in the second half of their lives (lives of service) have nothing to prove. They do what is right—helping others to be more intellectually and spiritually evolved—and let the universe take care of the rest.

The Mature Leader and the Golden Rule

People who feed their intellect and spirit, and the intellect and spirit of others, are living in accordance with the golden rule—a universal principle observed in all major religions. I particularly like the version from the Talmud:

> *What is hateful to you, do not unto your fellowman. That is the entire Law; all the rest is commentary.–Shabbat 31a.*

What is good for you is usually good for others. The rightness of this concept was demonstrated when my mother surrendered a few coins for a jubilant child to discover. My mother's reasoning was simple and just: "If it's good for me, it will be good for others." That is the golden rule.

The functioning of the heart is life sustaining. It nourishes our lives and the lives of all those we encounter. Employing all four chambers of the heart is the true measure of personal and professional success. You may believe that your vocation is to be a student, a spouse, a parent, an employee or boss. You are mistaken. Your vocation is to love; all the rest is commentary.

THE LANGUAGE OF LOVE

What does the language of love sound like? I submit that it is reflective of the four chambers of the heart: to learn, to be free, to teach, and to serve.

To Learn
- I know I don't know it all.
- I search out new experiences.
- I challenge my thinking.
- I can hardly wait to find out what I'm going to learn next.
- I learn by creating.
- Help me understand your point of view.
- I never saw it that way before; thank you.

To Be Free
- I do the right thing.
- I have nothing to prove to others.
- I am driven by a higher order.
- Having a deeper purpose, I can say no to the unimportant.
- I have nothing to prove, other than living by principles.
- Abiding by principles brings out the best in me.

To Teach
- How do you see the world?
- What are you passionate about?
- What works for you?
- What would you do differently next time?
- What if you tried this?

To Serve
- Talent, knowledge, and experience are terrible resources to waste.

- What is not given is lost.
- How can I help?
- How can I make a difference?
- What is my legacy?
- How can I serve you?
- My mission is to . . .

THE ACTIVITIES OF LOVE

What are the activities of love? How is love expressed? Here are a few suggestions presented as affirmations.

To Learn

- I seek activities that nourish my body, mind, heart, and soul; I take time for me.
- I am always learning something new, regardless of my age. (Verdi composed Falstaff—one of his most popular and demanding operas—at 80.)
- I immerse myself in a new course of study every three years.
- I read at least one book a month.
- I seek out experts for mentoring in fields that interest me.
- I create something new out of raw materials (a table, a painting, a short story, a vegetable garden).

To Be Free

- I consult with my conscience on tough decisions.
- I spend time in solitude.
- I meditate, pray, and read inspirational literature.
- I think twice about criticizing others.
- I laugh at myself because I have nothing to prove.

To Teach

- I model integrity.
- I listen wholeheartedly to others.
- I identify and connect with students who are ready to learn.

- I teach by helping others to discover new insight for themselves.
- I teach a Sunday school class, community class, scout troop.
- I coach a little league team, volleyball team, wrestling team.

To Serve

- I help others to be wiser, healthier, freer, more autonomous, and coach other servant leaders.
- I never squash the spirit and dreams of others.
- I make a difference in the lives of children.
- I create a men's or women's group.
- I volunteer my services as a speaker, leader, or tutor.
- I volunteer as a big brother or big sister.
- I host a foreign exchange student.

PUTTING LOVE TO WORK

The following questions are designed to help you access the quality of all four chambers of your love. Answering them will help you become a more loving individual.

To Learn

- What steps do I take toward being an active learner?
- How would I like to change or enhance my learning habits?

To Be Free

- In which relationships in my personal or professional life have I taken on the role of a persecutor, victim, or rescuer?
- What role did I play?
- What have been the consequences of taking that role?
- How would I prefer to behave?
- What would be the consequences of taking on this role?
- When and how will I introduce this more effective role?

To Teach

- What are my gifts (knowledge, skills, talents)?

- How could I share these gifts with others?

To Serve
- Who has given of themselves to help me mature and succeed?
- What did I learn from them (kindness, understanding, reason, discipline, patience, optimism)?
- Who would I like to help mature and succeed?
- What would I like them to learn from my example?

Chapter 6

THE DISCIPLINE OF RESPONSIBILITY

THE PATH OF CHOICE

We are responsible for actions performed in response to circumstances for which we are not responsible.

—Allan Massie

I had been counseling a woman once a week for about a month when one day she said, "Well, I've done it."

"What have you done?" I asked.

"I'm having an affair," the woman said. This was the first mention of an affair. "Tell me about it," I said.

The woman straightened her back in the leather wingchair as the hint of a smile formed on her lips. "I didn't mean for it to happen, " she said. "It was an accident."

Right. An affair may be a lot of things, I thought, but it certainly is not an accident.

•   •   •

If I were to observe you at home and at work for a week, what patterns would I see? What might I conclude about human behavior—that people are very simple-minded and predictable, simply responding to stimuli?

Are we little more than elegant robots, involuntarily responding to stimuli? I often ask people if they sometimes choose to not answer the phone. Most people occasionally choose to not answer the phone when it rings because . . .

"I'm tired, and want to be left alone."

"I know it's likely to be a telephone marketer."

"It won't be for me; it'll be for one of my kids."

"I'm soaking in the tub."

"It's dinner time, and that time is off limits to phone calls."

So, we are not controlled by stimuli; we are controlled by our needs. What do we want? Sometimes we want a moment of solitude, so we ignore the phone. Sometimes we want to satisfy our curiosity, and we answer the phone. Almost always we stop at red lights, because we need to safely arrive at our destination. But on occasion we may run the light to rush a loved one to the hospital or catch an early morning flight to that important meeting across the country. It is not the stimuli that drive us—it is our needs. Understanding this aspect of human behavior is pivotal in understanding the nature of responsibility.

DEFINING RESPONSIBILITY

I define *responsibility* as *the freedom to make principle-centered choices, regardless of the situation, through the employment of the five competencies, for the purpose of satisfying needs.* Let's break this definition down into four components: what, when, how, and why.

What: Freedom to make principle-centered choices. The freedom to make choices is our human heritage. What separates the responsible from the irresponsible is the nature of the choices selected. Responsible people select choices that are principle centered. A principle is a natural law, like gravity, that is universally and consistently true. In human relations, the test of a principle is the outcome it generates; behaviors that are principle-centered create richer, stronger relationships: more understanding, tolerance, love, forgiveness, and peace. Behavioral choices that are unprincipled are also recognized by the fruit they bare; they suck the blood out of relationships, making them smaller, more defensive, more alienated; the fruits are judgment, malice, vindictiveness.

When: Regardless of the situation. It is easy to behave responsibly when the conditions are favorable—when the sun is shining and all is right with the world; the real sign of maturity is the ability to act responsibly when the weather is stormy. Responsibility is not manifested when the car engine roars to life on the first twist of the ignition; it is manifested when the battery is dead. That is the test of responsibility—to face the challenges of the day with courage and dignity.

How: Through five human competencies. Five competencies—insight, moral knowledge, imagination, independent will, and self-transcendence—are the instruments of responsibility. These competencies are the power within that enable us to show kindness in the face of judgment, courage in the teeth of danger, and integrity in the rush of popular sentiment.

Why: To satisfy human needs. Friedrich Nietzsche said, "He who has a *why* to live for can bear with almost any *how*." How can we bear the weight of living responsibly? Through the *why* of human needs. The five competencies are the instruments—or skills—of responsibility, but human needs provide the motivation. Skill without motivation will always result in failure. Master technicians do not go to work every day because they possess the skill of the craft, but because their higher needs—self-worth, honor, power, freedom, and peace—are being satisfied.

The world has a proclivity for irresponsibility; more money is spent, more lives lost in the backlash of irresponsible behavior. Imagine what the world would be like if everyone abided by our definition of responsibility. There would be no need for police officers, soldiers, psychologists, or lawyers. But none of these professions will become obsolete anytime soon, because, unfortunately, most people often avoid or shortchange responsibility.

Repeatedly people tell me that they know what the right thing is to do; they are simply not able to do it. Why? What stops them? I suggest the problem is a broken cycle of principle-centered motivation (PCM). To engage responsibility, three things must happen: 1) the five competencies—the capacity skill set—must be highly developed, 2) the disciplines of effectiveness—the behavioral skill set—must be activated, and 3) the higher human needs—the motivating feelings—must be satisfied. If the cycle is broken, responsibility is in peril; if the cycle is unbroken, responsibility is secured.

The PCM cycle may be compared to the three steps in career development: 1) preparation—collect the raw resources: education, energy, ambition, goodwill; 2) application—do the work, attend the meetings, tackle the projects; 3) compensation—reap the benefits: earnings, satisfaction, or retirement.

The ultimate career motivation is the desire to satisfy the higher human needs (the compensation of self-worth, honor, power, freedom, peace). That goal is achieved though the preparation of human competencies (insight, moral knowledge, imagination, independent will, and self-transcendence) and the behavioral application of discipline (love, responsibility, vision, commitment, service).

Step 1 Human competencies The capacity skill set	Step 2 Disciplines of effectiveness The behavioral skill set	Step 3 Higher human needs The motivating feeling
Insight	Love (to learn)	Self-worth
Moral knowledge	Responsibility (to choose)	Honor
Imagination	Vision (to create)	Power
Independent will	Commitment (to act)	Freedom
Self-transcendence	Service (to contribute)	Peace

FIVE HIGHER NEEDS

The five higher needs—self-worth, honor, power, freedom, and peace—are different from the more basic survival or physical needs for food, water, and shelter. These higher needs provide the motivation for increased discipline.

Self-Worth. Self-worth is the product of the discipline of love, the will to extend one's self for the purpose of nurturing intellectual or spiritual growth for oneself and others. A sense of confidence emerges when we learn and when we share our knowledge with others. The payoff is increased confidence.

Honor. Honor is the product of the discipline of responsibility. Again, responsibility is the freedom to make principle-centered choices, regardless of the situation, for the purpose of satisfying human needs. When that is done—when we behave responsibly— a sense of honor is the outcome. Honor is defined as a steadfast allegiance to what is good and just.

Power. Power is the product of the discipline of vision. I define *power* not as the capacity to exercise control over others, but as the capacity to exercise control over one's self. Those who do not have a vision for themselves are at the mercy of those who do; personal power is, thus, handed over to the first "authority" with a vision. That is not power, it is abdication. A sense of power evolves when one is captured by his or her own vision.

Freedom. Freedom is the product of the discipline of commitment—the quality of independence from duplicitous influences. Freedom is not capricious; it is very disciplined in its commitment to behavior that is in alignment with one's highest-order vision of truth. The person who is committed to truth is unshackled from the domination of vanity and self-importance—that is true freedom: the freedom to be the best that one can be.

Peace. Peace is the product of the discipline of service. I define *peace* as serenity of mind and spirit. Peace evolves from service— from a dedication to nurturing the welfare and harmony of others. Self-satisfaction may come from gaining financial wealth, pride may come from earning accolades, but peace comes from service to others.

RESPONSIBILITY AND THE FIVE HIGHER NEEDS

Responsibility is hard work. Our natural tendency is to take the course of least resistance and to blame others for our misery. It is easy to fall into the trap of victimism, to be convinced that we do not have control of our own decisions, to believe that our condition in life is a product of an unhappy childhood, unfortunate marriage, or a dead-end job. Irresponsibility is continually reinforced in our language: "I can't help it; she really makes me mad; that really irritates me; he made me do it; I have no choice; I'm having a bad day; I got up on the wrong side of the bed; you drive me crazy."

We overcome irresponsibility by fulfilling our higher needs. Honor, the product of responsibility, promotes more responsibility. But honor, by itself, is insufficient. Responsibility takes the synergy of all five higher needs to transform the gristle of victimism into sinewy, moral muscle. The more we satisfy our higher needs, the more responsibly we behave.

APPLYING THE PCM CYCLE

Imagine that you wish to lose 20 pounds. This goal is frustrating to you, because you have failed so many times in the past. What must you do to succeed? Follow the five steps of the principle-centered motivation cycle.

1. Insight → Love → Self-worth → Insight

We all have the capacity to increase our level of insight and awareness of our surroundings. You might exercise that capacity by learning everything you can about weight loss. That effort—a manifestation of your love of self—will boost your self-worth. Why? You are more informed, more prepared for the task to come. Your sense of self-worth will nourish your capacity for insight; you will say to yourself, "I am more aware, and I have the capacity to learn even more."

2. Moral Knowledge → Responsibility → Honor → Moral Knowledge

Moral knowledge can play a role in losing 20 pounds. As ideas pop into our minds, moral knowledge enables us to sort out the grain from the chaff and make responsible, discriminating choices. What moral choices could possibly be associated with losing 20 pounds? Examine your motivation. Why do you want to lose the weight? To ensure your good health? To win the adoration of others? To impress old friends at the next class reunion. Or, perhaps, to deprive yourself of nourishment, for, after all, you are not worthy. If your choices are made for responsible reasons, you will enjoy the feeling of honor—the feeling that you have honored your highest ideals. The feeling of honor rests so comfortably in our souls that it calls us to listen even more earnestly to the voice of moral knowledge.

3. Imagination → Vision → Power → Imagination

Imagination is the capacity to make internal pictures. Vision enables us to filter those pictures to a precious, noble few. The *what* to do (lose 20 pounds for noble purposes) is supplied by the discipline of responsibility; the *how* to do it (our picture of the means and ends) is supplied by the discipline of vision. At this point you have satisfied yet another human need, the need for power—the capacity to exercise control over one's self. Power is the human need for centeredness, the sense that comes from feeling in control of our own destiny. Increased power stimulates greater imagination.

This makes intuitive sense. Think about the people you know who seem to be adrift, with little or no vision for themselves. Have you noticed that their imagination seems to be dried up? That arid landscape emerges from the underutilized competencies of insight, moral knowledge, and imagination.

4. Independent Will → Commitment → Freedom → Independent Will

The competency of independent will gives us the capacity to take bold steps to achieve our vision. That capacity is manifest in action through the discipline of commitment. Losing 20 pounds—or anything else, for that matter—is relatively easy when supported by insight, moral knowledge, and imagination. When we commit to a course of action, we satisfy the need for freedom. Without love, responsibility, and vision, we would be captives of our baser instincts: lust, jealousy, vindictiveness, hubris. But to commit to a carefully chosen mission frees us all. And that sense of freedom strengthens the competency of independent will.

5. Self-Transcendence →➤ Service →➤ Peace →➤ Self-Transcendence

Self-transcendence is the capacity to look beyond ourselves. How could losing 20 pounds help us tap that capacity to contribute to others? Meeting that goal might augment your energy, giving you the strength and desire to spend more time with the people you love: going for a walk, playing with the kids, going out of your way to care for a friend in need. Those actions spring from the discipline of service, and the outcome is the fulfillment of our need for peace. Inner peace feels so good that moving out of our own skin and into self-transcendence becomes our newly found place of comfort.

If you wish to lose 20 pounds—or resolve a conflict, find a satisfying job, discover personal truth, or anything else—live a life of responsibility by satisfying the five human needs.

The disciplines of personal effectiveness liberate us from the tyranny of pettiness, greed, self-indulgence, arrogance, and intolerance—anything that arrests the fulfillment of the higher human needs.

SELF-WORTH AS A PRODUCT OF INSIGHT AND LOVE

In 1971 I received my A1 draft status in the mail. I had been expecting it for months and, yet, still hoping that somehow it would not happen—that the war in Vietnam would end or that I would be deferred as a teacher or that I would be scrubbed out for some innocuous disease. But none of that happened. I knew what I had to do.

I have always abhorred guns. When I was 13 years old, my brother and I went hunting for pheasants in an open field along the river that belonged to a farmer who went to our church. I had an over-and-under Savage with a .22 caliber barrel over a 410 shotgun—pretty light weight as shotguns go. The brush my brother and I tramped through that day was nearly as tall as we were. The sun was hot on the back of my neck; threads of spider webs stuck to my face from all directions; suddenly, I knew that I did not want any part of this. At that moment the terrible and glorious sound of a pheasant taking flight made me jump out of my skin.

"Get 'im," my brother yelled.

Just to the right and 10 yards out, a missile of brown feathers was flying just above the brush and into the sun. I lifted the Savage to my shoulder, pointed, closed my eyes, and pulled the trigger. The brown bird tumbled to the ground. I moved forward quickly through the brush. There it lay, one wing folded over its head. I knelt down beside the bird, afraid to touch it. I poked at it with the mussel of my gun. It did not move. I lay the gun down and picked up the bird with both hands. Its body was warm in my hands; its head hung limp. Noting that it was a hen pheasant, I was suddenly filled with shame and remorse (the same feeling I saw in the eyes of my brother a few days earlier when he eyeballed a robin in a tree overhead, picked up a smooth stone, took aim, and, unbelievably, knocked the bird off its perch). Quickly, I dug a shallow grave for the bird with the stock of my gun.

I stood up. There were tears in my eyes. I called out to my brother: "Ray, I'm going home."

"Did you get the bird?" my brother asked.

"I couldn't find him," I said.

"Let's keep looking," my brother shot back.

I said nothing and walked out of the field.

That was the last time that I have ever shot a gun.

I was in graduate school at the University of Washington when I got my draft notice. The next day I spotted a hand-drawn poster stapled to a bulletin board outside the library. I followed the map to a center for conscientious objectors located in an old, two-story, Victorian house two blocks off campus. I walked up the wooden porch steps. The front door was open. Just to the left of the entry way was a card table, covered with copies and tri-fold brochures. A young man in faded blue jeans and a red madras shirt rocked on the back two legs of a metal folding chair behind the table. His long, blond hair was tied back into a ponytail, held in place with a rubber band. He seemed incredibly street smart.

I felt nervous. I kept telling myself I was doing the right thing, but, still, I had all those tapes of John Wayne movies doing battle in my head. The man in the ponytail seemed like the antithesis of everything American heroes stood for.

When I approached the table, he let his chair lower to all fours. "What can I do for you?" he asked. My eyes gazed at the handouts and brochures on the card table. I didn't know where to start—even what question to ask. The man smiled, revealing a perfect set of teeth. "Hey, don't let it overwhelm you. We're just friends here. Let's start with this." The man put a brochure in my hand. "Why don't you read that, and then come back. I'll answer any questions you might have."

The man in the ponytail was a wealth of information. I learned about the process of requesting CO status, about fielding questions that draft boards ask, about finding an alternate service. The more I learned, the more my confidence grew. Suddenly I felt reassured. I was not alone. There were others who were struggling with the same dilemma: how to serve their country without taking the life of another human being.

By the time I faced my draft board, I had no reservations. I had done my homework. I looked them straight in the eyes. "I am a conscientious objector. I cannot in good conscience take arms against another."

One of the broad members—an ex-marine, I learned later—cleared his throat. "What if everyone thought like you?"

"Sir," I said, "there would be no wars."

"Do you believe that could ever happen?" the marine asked.

"No, sir, I do not. But that, I believe, is beside the point. I cannot speak for the choices other young Americans make. I can only say that I have the responsibility to abide by my conscience, and must act accordingly. Every other young man has that same right; whether they take it or not is totally up to them."

The marine was silent. Three days later I received notice that my CO status was granted on the condition that I fulfill my alternate service with the Mennonite Central Committee—exactly as I had outlined to the draft board.

I was just beginning to understand the cycle of insight/love/self-worth. That fall, my wife Nita and I packed our bags for a three-year interim in our careers. The first year we lived in Grenoble, France and studied French. The last two years we taught high school English in a small mountain village in Northern Algeria. Our salary: room, board, and $25 a month.

In those three years, insight buzzed around us like a storm of angry bees. The adjustment was difficult, particularly the first year. At the time, I did not know the expression "cultural shock," but I certainly experienced it. Our apartment in Grenoble had a coat of rancid grease on all surfaces and a shower drain that smelled like the port to the city sewer. Three days after our arrival, Nita wrote these words in her journal:

> 9.25.71. I was all weepy today. The apartment is an unbelievable mess, the smells are nauseating, my stomach felt awful. Made soup, which was like paste. I haven't the hang of their measuring system. Spent the afternoon walking downtown, trying to figure out what I was doing here. Sure I wanted to see Europe, maybe even live here, but by American standards. I guess I am just too American. I want to learn the language and be friends, but I am finding it hard to adjust to the stares and smells. Al got pretty upset with me early in the day, because I felt so low, which didn't help me any. I guess he was fighting depression himself, and I wasn't helping him.

I remember that day clearly. We were both in shock, stunned by the newness of our surroundings and, by virtue of our pigeon French, our humbling regression to infancy. I felt completely disoriented and angry about everything, particularly my inability to communicate. My wife and I had been married for nearly three years, and that day was the first time I had barked at her. "You've got to get it together," I snapped. "We're gonna do this thing. But you've got to help me; I need you to be strong—and I'll try to be strong for you."

That was the first step toward insight: being aware of what we were feeling. We knew we had a lot to learn. That night we set up a plan of attack. Notice the shift in tone in Nita's journal.

9.26.71. We got up early and started cleaning. Al put boards on the bed upstairs, and it actually doesn't feel too bad. He hung curtains, while I scrubbed and tried to get rid of some of the dirt and smell. The place is built like a town house, and if you could paint, hang pictures, put down rugs, etc., it wouldn't be half bad. We have a study, a bedroom, and a shower upstairs; a living room, dining room/kitchen combination, and a balcony downstairs. The drain in the shower still stinks, but we will look for a plug tomorrow and keep it plugged except when in use.

9.27.71. Monday morning. It was easy to get up today. Not afraid to face the realities of the day. Had bread and hot chocolate for breakfast. Found a store that sold mops, Clorox, and drain plugs. Had an interesting time getting across what we wanted. The plug seems to be keeping the smell down. Mopped for a couple of hours. Al did the upstairs mopping. We went for a walk and bought a fern. Had steak, French fries, and salad for dinner. We both thought it was delicious. A good day.

When we began to open our hearts and minds to our new home, we began to grow. We began to learn, and with knowledge came confidence. When someone asks me how he or she can be more confident, my response is this: "Forget about being more confident. Go for being more competent—the rest will follow."

HONOR AS A PRODUCT OF MORAL KNOWLEDGE AND RESPONSIBILITY

In 1962, when I was a sophomore in high school, my parents drew up their last will and testament. It was very simple. Upon their death all their worldly goods would be divided equally between their two sons.

Thirty-four years later my mom and dad asked me to drop by the house to talk about a revision to their will.

Mom took the lead. "Son, we have decided that when we die all our resources will be divided equally among our grandchildren and great-grandchildren." (Mom was talking about my brother's children and grandchildren; Nita and I have no kids.) "We know that you are financially secure. We don't worry about you. But we think our grandchildren and their families could use a jump start in life."

I felt a twitch in my stomach as though something in me had just been jump started.

"What do you think, Son?" Mom asked.

"Let me get this straight," I said with a crooked smile, "I'm out of the will."

My father laughed. "Yeah, I guess that's about it."

"What do you think?" my mom asked again.

"I think that what is important to me is that you do what is important to you."

Mom smiled. "Thank you, Son."

I looked at Dad. He was very still—expressionless. That was unlike him; he usually was more expressive when it comes to matters involving money.

"Of course, if you had children," Mom added, "they, too, would have been included."

"Gee," I said with a half smile, "I'll have to double check and make sure that I haven't sired a few that I don't know about." We all pretended to laugh. I still felt the twitch in my stomach, and I noticed that my breathing was shallow—something was not right. I gave my parents a hug, wishing them a good day.

As I drove home I felt half sick. I was ashamed of myself. Intellectually, I agreed with my folks wholeheartedly. It was true, we were financially secure; it certainly did make sense to help the third and fourth generations who were just starting out. But I still felt empty. What was it?

That evening a men's group I had founded a year earlier gathered in my office for one of our biweekly meetings. I told them what had happened that day.

"I just feel disappointed in myself," I said.

"How do you want to feel?" Larry asked.

Larry always asks questions that cut right to the chase.

"I want to celebrate my parent's decision," I said. "I really do, and yet I feel I have been denied my birthright. It is not about the money; it really isn't. It's something else."

"I know the feeling," someone else said. "Years ago my best friend had an affair with my ex-wife. Last week he had the nerve to leave a message on my machine, asking if I would like to get together with him and another old buddy and reminisce. My first impulse was to say, 'no damn way.' Then I thought, 'I have to forgive him.' He called again three days ago. I'm going to return his call. It's the right thing to do."

"I think you are looking for something symbolic," Larry said.

"What do you mean?"

"I think you are looking for some symbolic passage from father to son. I don't know how you will do that; I don't know what is meaningful for you. I think that is something you will have to figure out for yourself."

Damn, that Larry is good.

That night I went to bed early. Around midnight I was awakened by a thought. I knew what I wanted. I was absolutely clear on what I had to do.

I got up at 5:30 in the morning. I knew Ray was an early riser and so I called him.

"Ray, are you in town today?"

"Yeah."

My brother has a practice of visiting our parents in the morning. "Are you going to see Mom and Dad today."

"Yeah. Probably around seven."

"I'll be there," I said quickly and immediately hung up.

An hour and a half later I walked through the door into my folk's living room. Ray was already there. I wanted him to know that everything was all right, so I squeezed his shoulder as I walked past him and found a seat on the couch. There we were, the four of us, just like the old days.

I started by reviewing what Mom and Dad had said the previous day. The room was dead still; they were waiting for what was going to come next. I decided to set their minds at rest immediately. "Mom and Dad, I think your decision is terrific. Pass whatever resources you have to those who are in greatest need. Maybe earmark some of it for their education—that is the best way that they can move ahead."

"Thank you, Son," Mom said. Dad and Ray were frozen. They were waiting for the other shoe to drop.

"But you know what? I felt a kind of emptiness when I left yesterday, and I couldn't quite put my finger on it. Last night it came to me. It's this: I want your blessing—a benediction. If you are willing, I would like you to stand before family and friends and invoke God's favor for me and my brother. I would like a ceremony, a kind of sacrament, where you place your hands on my head and Ray's head and say . . ." I was suddenly welling up with emotion. I paused for a moment; no one said a word. "Where you say, 'These are our sons, in whom we are well pleased.' That's the only inheritance I want."

"Oh, Son," Mom said, "what a wonderful idea. I understand. I am only sorry that we didn't think of it." Then turning to Dad, she said, "Honey, what do you think?"

"I don't know if Allen knows this," my Dad said, "but I pray for him every day. I want God's best for him, but if he would like me to say that in public, I will. Gladly. I have not always treated you right, Allen. I have not always treated Ray right. And I hope you forgive me for that. I have nothing but love for you both."

I reached out my hand to my father. "I do, Dad. That is over, that is way behind us."

"What do you think, Son?" Mom said to Ray.

Ray was quiet for a moment. He shrugged and readjusted himself in the chair by the door. "I am very passive about this. The money is not important to me."

I nodded in agreement.

"What is important," Ray continued, "is how we treat each other today. We can ask for a blessing from others, that's fine, but what are we doing to bless others. That's the question. We have to make certain that we are demonstrating our love, before we are gone. None of us is immortal. All of us will die someday." Then with a half smile, he made reference to the stroke he had a year earlier: "For a while there I thought it was going to be me sooner than the rest." He paused for a moment. "I had a friend who was killed in a motorcycle accident last week. I can tell you that death was the last thing on his mind on that day. We never know. We've got to love each other today."

In a moment we all stood. I gave Ray a hug. Dad came over and put his arms around both of us. "I love you both, you big palookas," he said, which made Ray laugh. And then Mom came and we had a family hug.

Ray and I walked out of the house together. "How long are you in town?" Ray asked.

"Until Sunday," I said.

He smiled. "I'll give you a call sometime this week."

"Good. I'll look forward to that."

Ray got into his pickup, I got into my car, and we drove away.

That same day, upon my mother's request, I penned the following invitation:

> *Helen and Thurston Johnson wish to invite you to a special celebration: A day of benediction to bless our sons, Allen and Ray, before God, family, and our dearest friends.*
>
> *The ceremony—an evening of love, forgiveness, and blessing—will be conducted at 6 o'clock PM on Monday, November 25, 1996, at Faith Assemble Church located on Court Street and Road 72 in Pasco, Washington.*
>
> *In the tradition of earlier days, there will be a potluck feast immediately after the ceremony. (Please bring your favorite casserole, salad, or dessert.) Please join us for this celebration of love and family.*
> *RSVP*

That celebration never happened—not formally. The next day my brother called me early in the morning. "Allen, I thought about your idea for a celebration of benediction."

I knew what was coming.

"I can't do it," my brother said. "I know that you feel comfortable with that sort of thing, but I'm not that way. I'm not feeling that good about myself these days; it's just not something I can do."

I understood. Ray had gone through a lot in the last year. "That's okay," I said. "I'm disappointed—I thought it would be a great evening of love and celebration—but it's okay. I understand."

Two days later my mom called me. "Allen, we've been thinking about our will again, and we've decided to leave it as it stands: Whatever we leave will be divided equally among our two sons."

"Mom," I protested, "that's not what I wanted."

"I understand," Mom said. "It's what we want. We don't know what we were thinking. You and Ray are good boys. You will know how to use the money. Okay? I love you. And Allen . . ."

"Yeah, Mom."

"You are my son, in whom I am well pleased."

I tell that story with a sense of peace. I believe that my moral knowledge was accessed as soon as I recognized the angst of feeling one thing ("a twitch in my gut") while saying something else ("what is important to me is that you do what is important to you"). By the next morning I had used the resource of moral knowledge to make my decision—an act of responsibility. I felt that choice was honorable, a choice built on what was truly important: the relationship.

I believe that my parents and my brother also sought wisdom from their consciences. In the end, my parents wished to honor the wisdom of their sons. My brother sought to underscore the importance of being a blessing, as opposed to just being blessed. I think those sentiments come from the seat of moral knowledge, but, in the final analysis, it does not matter what I think; what matters is what they think—if, indeed, they have wrestled through the night with the source of divine truth, and allowed truth to win out.

POWER AS A PRODUCT OF IMAGINATION AND VISION

When I was 45 years old, I wrote a personal, principle-centered mission statement, a kind of constitution for myself. It was a formal declaration of my behavioral intentions. A pivotal sentence in that statement was this: *I live a life of dignity and integrity, regardless of the circumstances.*

One week after writing those words, my resolve was put to the test. I was traveling across the country on business. On my route home, I had to change planes in Salt Lake City. Because my incoming flight was delayed, I had to run from one end of the terminal to the other to catch the connecting flight home. I had only 10 minutes to make it. If I missed my plane, I would be forced to spend the night lounging in the airport.

I ran down the moving sidewalk—a four-foot wide conveyer belt with protective railing on either side—grasping a shoulder bag with one hand and my business planner with flight ticket in the other. As I sprinted down the runway I called out to the people ahead.

"Please let me pass. Please let me pass."

Courteously, all the travelers moved to the right as I hurried past them to my gate. All, I should say, except for one. A single, tall businessman in a dark suit and brief case in hand stood his ground.

The closer I got to him, the louder I called out. "Please let me pass. SIR, PLEASE LET ME PASS."

Still, the man would not budge. In fact, I saw him actually pull back and brace his shoulders, as if determined to hold his ground, no matter what.

When I came along side, I tried to force my way around his left. At that instant the man lowered his left shoulder and, incredibly, rammed me into the railing. The move was something you might see in a hockey match, but not in an international airport.

"Oh, brother," I said under my breath, and continued my race for the gate.

I had taken two or three steps when the man called out to me. "Hey, buddy, you dropped your ticket."

I looked at my right hand. Sure enough, my flight ticket had fallen out of my business planner. I turned back and saw the ticket resting beside the foot of the man who had just leveled me with a body check.

Reluctantly, I turned back to where the man was standing. I knelt down to pick up my ticket. And that's when I did it; that's when I violated my principles. I said, "You know, mister, you've really got to learn to give in a little."

That would not have been so bad—although the statement was certainly parental in word and tone, and intended to be punishing. The subtext was, "Let me take a moment out of my day to make you a better person"—not a healthy approach when standing nose to nose with a hockey player. The trouble was, I did not stop there. I cannot tell you what I said next. Let's just say I offered a sordid description of the man's mental capacity.

When I tell this story, people instinctively laugh at this point. That is understood. It is an expression of the rebellious child in all of us—that small voice cries out, "Get even!"

With my arrow flung, and my target left bleeding, I stood and resumed my sprint to the gate. I had taken one step forward, when the tall businessman leaned back and let loose with a kick to my backside. I had black and blue marks the shape of a size 12 oxford on my caboose for a week and a half to prove it.

I said nothing. I was absolutely determined to make my flight on time. And I was successful. Last call was being announced just as I reached the gate.

As I settled in my seat I reflected on the incident. The kick to the pants was not nearly as painful as what I was telling myself: Allen, you messed up. You violated your principles. I live a life of dignity and integrity—regardless of the circumstances. Right. Suddenly I felt as though my conscience became flesh and grabbed me by the throat. I surveyed the people around me, hoping that someone would behave rudely to me, so I might have a chance to redeem myself. In the words of Ernest Hemingway, I wanted the chance to prove I had the grit to live a life with "grace under pressure."

My chance came several weeks later. I was playing basketball with some schoolteachers and administrators one Saturday morning.

Now, I love to play basketball. You give me an evenly matched game of three-on-three half court and I'm in macho heaven. Oh, yes—I'm also very competitive, and an occasional poor sport.

My opponent, we'll call him Jerry, was also very competitive— and, like me, a little out of control. At one point in the game, Jerry was dribbling down center court. He looked to his right to pass the ball. I realized he had lost sight of me, so I planted my feet and braced myself, knowing he was bound to crash into me. The unexpected collision decked him. Now, if the defender's feet are set and the offensive player runs into him, it is a charging foul on the offensive player. That was exactly what happened in this case. I was right; he was wrong.

However, that was not the way Jerry saw it. He leapt to his feet, began shoving me in the chest, and made disparaging remarks regarding the legitimacy of my birth and the virtue of my mother.

At that instant my mission statement leapt to mind. What are you going to do, Allen? I asked myself. I looked Jerry straight in the eyes and said calmly and simply, "My feet were set. You were charging."

Again Jerry launched into another barrage of insults.

I simply turned and walked away.

I glowed for the next two weeks. Not because I had something to prove to Jerry, but because I had something to prove to myself: to live by a vision of integrity and dignity. It just felt good to do the right thing.

The discipline of vision is the act of creating a picture of our destination that is worthy of pursuit. Writing a mission statement (and committing it to memory) is a crucial step in living a life of vision. The advantage is this: With time your responses become more and more a reflection of your mission. Soon, the impulse to win, or get revenge, is replaced with the decision to do the right thing. The more we substitute honorable decisions for impulse, the more powerful we become.

Freedom as a Product
of Independent Will and Commitment

It was 7:30 in the morning. I was on my way to work and feeling spunky. I was driving the Corvette, a sportscar I no longer own. That is probably a good thing because something electric happened when I settled in behind the wheel of that car and looked over the broad hood that sloped down and out of sight.

I came to a rolling stop at a busy intersection. I needed to make a right-hand turn. I looked to my left. There was a vehicle barreling down the road at high speed. In that instant I had to decide: do I wait or do I punch it? I said to myself, "I'm in my Corvette; I'll just punch it."

After I scooted around the corner and zoomed down the straightaway, I glanced at my rear-view mirror. The driver flashed his lights at me.

"Yep," I said to myself, "I cut that one a little too close."

I stopped at the next intersection to make a left turn. I waited for the oncoming traffic to clear. Meanwhile, I checked my rear-view mirror again. It was a woman in a four-wheel drive pickup truck with a gun rack and a bumper sticker that read *Goat Ropers Need Love Too*. The pickup was jacked up and hovering over the Vette like a rain cloud. The woman's teeth were snapping, and her hands were making menacing circles in the air.

I have this principle that I try to live by. When I am at fault, I apologize. I tried to relay that message to the woman in the pickup: I hunched my shoulders and screwed my right index finger into my right temple—the universal sign for stupidity. Unfortunately, that particular gesture does not clearly designate who, exactly, is the stupid person in question.

Judging by the steamed expression of the woman in my mirror, she thought the "stupid sign" was meant for her. It was not. What is the right thing to do in such a case? For me it meant making a clear apology.

So, I opened the door to the Corvette, stepped out, and walked back to the pickup. Her window was rolled down. Her eyes were inflamed, and she was just about to speak, when I said, "You are absolutely right. I was dead wrong. I apologize."

The woman said nothing. She could not have looked more surprised. I pivoted, got back into the Vette, and drove away.

I suspect that if the woman in the pickup truck were interviewed, she might say: "Sure, I'm ticked. He cut me off. Look at him; he's a raving idiot."

I, on the other hand, felt something entirely different: a sense of freedom. I had exercised my loyalty to personal principles, and that made me free. Why? I was not a victim of the woman's rancor. There is no greater freedom than choosing not to be a victim of unfortunate circumstances.

PEACE AS A PRODUCT
OF SELF-TRANSCENDENCE AND SERVICE

One of my best friends is Terry Barber, an elementary school principal. This is his story.

It was the end of the school day. Terry was on duty, helping the youngsters to board buses for home. One of the teachers asked Terry for some help; a third-grade boy was "cursing up a storm." The assistant pointed the way.

Terry walked quickly to where the boy was standing. He placed his left hand on the boy's shoulder and pointed his finger at him. He used his all-business, principal's voice: "We do not allow cursing on our school grounds. Is that understood, young man?"

The boy locked his jaw and nodded that he understood.

A half-hour later, Terry opened the front door of the school to leave. At that very moment, the father of the third-grade boy met Terry at the door. Terry held the door open for the man. Without any fanfare, the man grabbed Terry with both hands by his shirt collar, pushed him back into the school and slammed him into a bank of lockers. Terry—weighing 140 pounds on a humid day—was no match for the six-foot-four man, who, as Terry was to discover later, was a convicted killer. The man handled Terry like a rag doll. He picked Terry up and threw him a distance of 10 feet against the wall on the opposite side of the hallway.

The man stood over Terry and showed his eight-year-old son (who was standing in shock behind him) how a real man curses. For some reason—surprisingly, fortunately—the man did not continue the assault.

The school secretary rushed out of the office into the hallway.

"Call the police," Terry said.

"Yeah, call the police," the man said. "Put this son-of-a-bitch in jail."

Terry managed to stand up. Slowly he maneuvered his way toward the office. His intention, as he explained to me later, was to be the buffer between this enraged man and his office staff.

Terry said nothing as the man lashed out in fury—his anger the product of an outrageous lie (the boy had told his father that Terry had punched and strangled him). The blue veins in the man's neck were pulsating, his hands clenched into fists at his sides.

Still, Terry said nothing. But he did listen intently.

Four minutes later the police arrived. Calmly and without force they led the man into an empty room. Terry was directed to stay in his office. An hour later the man was handcuffed and taken away in a squad car.

Four days after the incident, Terry and his wife, Pat, were at our home for dinner. It was then that Terry told the story.

"You want to know the strangest thing about all this?" Terry asked. "Throughout it all I was never fearful; I knew that he could do great harm, but I was not afraid; I felt perfectly calm. My heart didn't race, and I never got the shakes. I felt as if I were out of my body and observing the whole thing—completely detached."

"How do you explain that?" I asked.

"I don't know. Cognitively I can't explain it. But spiritually, it's easy to explain."

Terry didn't elaborate. He didn't have to; I knew what he meant already. I think that Terry was at peace because he is a man of peace. As long as I have known Terry, nearly 25 years now, he has always been an advocate for peace: settling professional disputes amicably, coaching students on the peaceful resolution of differences, writing letters of compassion on the behalf of political and spiritual prisoners around the world. He is a secular (not ordained) member of the Franciscan order, whose mission is to abide by the teachings of Christ, particularly the Sermon on the Mount and the Beatitudes. He begins every school day by broadcasting the following benediction to all classrooms:

I will be a peaceful person.
I will make my world a more peaceful place.
I will set a peaceful example for others to follow.

"Being peaceful is hard work," Terry once told me. "I pray that my soul be filled with love so that I may transform my acre of land."

"What do you mean by your *acre of land*?" I asked.

"My acre of land is wherever I am at the moment," Terry explained, "whatever potential for influence I have."

Terry strives to transcend his personal desires. Throughout his life he has sought to serve others, particularly to help youngsters become mature, responsible citizens. Acting on that calling has created a sense of peace for Terry—an ability, for example, to remain calm in the face of eminent danger. But his actions have also ignited a desire for peace in the lives of those who stand on his acre of land: students, parents, friends, and family. I, too, have been touched by his example.

THE TIMING OF RESPONSIBILITY

I was in Denver on business, but I hoped to weave in a visit with my cousin who lived in Arvada, a Denver suburb. After I checked in a hotel, I sought out the concierge. He was a young man in his late twenties and, as I was soon to find out, well suited for his position.

"Excuse me," I said.

"Yes, sir, how may of be of service?" The young man's words were offered precisely, but with a tone of sincerity that is often lacking in positions of customer service.

"Could you please tell me how many miles it is to Arvada?" I asked.

The concierge smiled. "What time are you going?"

For whatever reason—blame it on a long day of traveling—I responded sarcastically. "Does the mileage change, depending on the time of day?"

The young man was unruffled. "No, sir, it's just that the traffic may slow your progress during rush hour. To answer your question, Arvada is approximately 15 miles away. If the traffic is light you would be able to get there in 20 to 30 minutes."

"Thank you."

"You are entirely welcome," the young man said, still without a hint of malice or pretense.

I took a step away and then stopped dead in my tracks. What was I doing? Why was I being rude to a man who sought only to serve? It was not right. I turned around and faced the young concierge again. "Excuse me, I have to apologize for my behavior. Just a moment ago I made a sarcastic remark that was totally uncalled for. You were nothing but kind. I'm sorry."

"Oh, I didn't notice, sir."

"Well, it doesn't matter. This is really more about me than it is about you. I'm generally not short with people, and it is not a habit I want to start picking up."

"Think nothing of it, sir. Anytime I can be of service, please call."

In being responsible, timing is everything. There are really three moments in time when one can choose to be responsible:

The present. One can choose to behave responsibly at the present moment, to stop in mid-sentence and say, "You know what, I just messed up. What I just said was not right; let me start again."

The future. One can choose to be responsible after the event. My apology to the young concierge is an example. Responsible behavior that occurs after the event is not nearly as hearty as responsible behavior that occurs during the event. Still, in Denver I did not wait too long—perhaps 30 seconds. I would have been less responsible if I had waited until the next day, and not responsible at all if I had ignored the opportunity altogether.

The past. The greatest moment of responsibility is born before the event. What if I were so mature—so grounded in the human competencies and disciplines of effectiveness—that I never behaved irresponsibly at the moment of challenge? That is real responsibility: the silent samurai who is so spiritually centered and so physically confident that he remains perfectly calm, even serene, in the face of danger.

Truly responsible people are supremely centered. That centeredness does not come by chance; it comes through the unbroken fulfillment of the cycle of principle-centered motivation. Consequently, their human needs—self-worth, honor, power, freedom, and peace—are abundantly satisfied; they can be naturally serene, for they have nothing to prove—they have it all already.

THE LANGUAGE OF RESPONSIBILITY

What do responsible people say? What they don't say is "I can't, I'll try, I can't help it, I have no choice." What they do say follows:

- I create my own destiny.
- I am angering, depressing, miserablizing (taking personal responsibility for my own feelings).
- I've decided to . . .
- I choose to . . .
- That's not like me. Let me start again.
- My behavior was inappropriate. I am going to do everything in my power to see that it doesn't happen again.
- I am at fault.
- I was wrong.
- I support your decision in doing the right thing. And if you don't know what the right thing is, let's talk about it.

THE ACTIVITIES OF RESPONSIBILITY

What do responsible people do? They certainly don't sit idle, nor do they spend their time confessing the sins of others.

The following is a modest sampling of their actions:

- I look at myself through a third eye and monitor the appropriateness of my behavior.
- I connect to my mission, clarify roles and goals, plan weekly, and practice making the right choices daily.
- I spend time in my deep inner life (it builds my responsibility "muscles").
- I write letters of gratitude.
- I write letters of forgiveness.
- I investigate my options and seek out the opinions of others.
- I offer to make amends for my errors.
- I clarify goals and expectations.
- I accept my failures and seek to learn from them.
- I convert good intentions into actions.
- I practice being of service to others.

PUTTING RESPONSIBILITY TO WORK

One can begin to build strength in responsibility by attending to a situation that is difficult or perplexing or by mending a relationship that is broken. How can you improve the situation or heal the relationship? One strategy is to begin by considering the personal, higher-order needs you would like to satisfy; getting a sense of how you would like to feel after a difficult encounter. The following open-ended statements can help in designing that strategy.

Self-worth. I would feel better about myself if I . . . [Describe what you need to learn as a result of resolving the situation.]

Honor. Of all the options available, the most honorable is . . . [Describe the option of choice that aligns with your conscience.]

Power. I feel a sense of legitimate power (dominion over my own destiny), when I picture myself . . . [Describe a picture of the final outcome—the more detailed, the better.]

Freedom. I am free to do a lot of things, but the noblest steps to take in this situation are . . . [Describe the action steps you plan to take that are congruent with your conscience.]

Peace. I will be at peace with myself if I . . . [Describe the positive contribution that your action will make in the lives of those involved.]

Chapter 7

THE DISCIPLINE OF VISION

THE PATH OF NOBILITY AND REVOLUTION

> *"Would you tell me, please, which way I ought to go from here?"*
> *Alice speaks to Cheshire Cat.*
> *"That depends on where you want to get to," said the Cat.*
> *"I don't much care where—" said Alice.*
> *"Then it doesn't matter which way you go," said the Cat.*
>
> —Lewis Carroll

A re you familiar with the name Craig Keilburger? On May 2, 1998, Craig and his organization were awarded the Franklin Eleanor Roosevelt Freedom from Fear Award. (The three other recipients were African Archbishop Desmond Tutu; Mary Robinson, the United States High Commissioner for Human Rights; and Stéphane Hessel, French diplomat.) Craig has addressed some of the most prestigious forums of the world: United States Congressional Committees, the Correspondents' Association of the United Nations, the World Congress on Family Law, and the State of the World Forum. To advance his cause he has traveled to all corners of the world—from Brazil to Thailand, from Sweden to Kenya. He has met with and been praised by heads of states and religious leaders, including the Dalai Lama and Pope John Paul II. Add to his credits a best selling autobiography.

Who is this person? An industrial magnate? A president or prime minister? Perhaps a religious leader of world stature. No. Craig Keilburger is a schoolboy from Toronto, Canada.

In April 1995, when Craig was 12 years old, he was searching his local paper for the funnies. Instead, what caught his eye was a story about a Pakistani child who was sold into slavery by his parents when the child was four years old. Until his escape, six years later, the boy worked 12 hours a day, six days a week, tying knots at a carpet loop. When the Pakistani boy exposed his story and the evil of child labor to the media, there was a financial backlash for the carpet industry; the boy was murdered.

Craig was set on fire by that story. He began by communicating with human rights organizations to find out everything he could about child labor. He created Free the Children, a human rights organization led by Craig and his classmates with a four-part charter:

1. To create a greater awareness of child labor and the exploitation of children.
2. To convince world leaders to make child education and protection a priority.
3. To raise funds to aid exploited or abused children.
4. To collaborate with children around the world to help generate change.

While still 12 years old, Craig convinced his parents to allow him to visit five countries in Asia—Bangladesh, Thailand, India, Nepal, and Pakistan—to see for himself the realities of child exploitation. He saw it all: an eight-year-old barefoot girl whose job was to recycle bloody syringes, children working in extremely dangerous fireworks factories, and even children sold for sex on the streets. You can read about Craig's experience in his book *Free the Children*.

Begun in 1995, Craig's campaign has been in high gear ever since. Through his influence, the Canadian government donated $700,000 to the International Program for the Elimination of Child Labor and took measures to ensure that products imported into the country were not manufactured through the exploitation of children. Craig has taken great advantage of the mass media, with interviews on "60 Minutes," CNN International, The Voice of America, and the Italian "Maurizui Costanzo Show." Add to all that his frequent exposure as an international keynote speaker and founder of the annual, six-day, international Free the Children Convention. One of his messages at those events is that children can and must make a difference in world affairs. His fervor is paying off; there are Free the Children chapters around the world. What more can we expect from this Canadian schoolboy?

•   •   •

A vision of substance must have two ingredients: a principle-centered core of nobility, and a revolutionary design. Historian Daniel J. Boorstin has offered two examples from American history.

In June of 1776, Thomas Jefferson drafted the *Declaration of Independence*. It was, of course, adopted by the Continental Congress on the next month, July 4, 1776. The ideas were not new—they had been expounded by John Locke and other continental philosophers—but the results were revolutionary. The heart of the document was captured in this eloquent phrase:

> *We hold these truths to be self-evident, that all men are created equal, that they are endowed by their Creator with certain unalienable Rights, that among these are Life, Liberty and the pursuit of Happiness.*

That sentence leaps out as the founders' commitment to a "core of nobility"—self-evident principles. But the declaration did not end there. It went on to state its revolutionary intent:

Whenever any Form of Government becomes destructive of these ends, it is the Right of the People to alter or to abolish it, and institute new Government, laying its foundation on such principles and organizing its powers in such form, as to them shall seem most likely to effect their safety and happiness.

That sentence captures the revolutionary nature of the founders' vision. It is a sentence with teeth in it as deadly as colonial bayonets. It is a statement that is as much a death warrant as it is a declaration of independence, for to sign the statement was an act of high treason against the King of Great Britain. It was truly revolutionary.

Abraham Lincoln reclaimed the words of the *Declaration of Independence* when he consecrated a cemetery for Union soldiers in Gettysburg, Pennsylvania on November 19, 1863:

Four score and seven years ago our fathers brought forth on this continent a new nation, conceived in Liberty, and dedicated to the proposition that all men are created equal.

Lincoln's next sentence connects that noble idea of liberty and equality with the tenacity of pursuit, for, surely, a vision of nobility requires a heavy commitment—even a commitment as dear as a horrific civil war:

Now we are engaged in a great civil war, testing whether that nation, or any nation so conceived and so dedicated, can long endure.

Lincoln ended the famous address by answering his own question with resounding resolution:

... that this nation, under God, shall have a new birth of freedom — and that government of the people, by the people, for the people, shall not perish from the earth.

Both of these historic examples demonstrate the duality of great vision: a commitment to principles, so passionate that the visionary is willing, if necessary, to pursue that cause with revolutionary fervor—to take on the opposition, to fly in the face of traditional wisdom, to put one's reputation, even one's life, on the line for truth and virtue.

And if, in time, the virtue of action should come into question, it is time to rethink the situation and, perhaps again, become revolutionary in one's vision. I return to Gettysburg for an example.

Nearly 50,000 men were killed or wounded in the Gettysburg campaign, 13,000 in Pickett's charge alone. In that battle the Confederate troops marched across the rolling open fields of Gettysburg. The Union soldiers waited on the boundary, protected by the woods. Then, with the Confederate soldiers 200 yards away, the federal troops opened fire. Entire southern regimens were destroyed in one volley. It was the single most tragic event of the war.

On the 50th anniversary of that battle, there was a reunion of the Gettysburg veterans. The highlight of the gathering was a reenactment of Pickett's charge. When the old men of the Confederate army approached their enemy, a long sigh was heard among the Union veterans. Those old warriors could not take it any longer; they stood up from their hiding places and ran out to their former enemies and embraced them as brothers. Perhaps forgiveness is the most revolutionary of actions.

DEFINING VISION

Vision has two components: nobility and revolution.

Many people have pursued ignoble visions—the dictators, tyrants, and bullies of the world—but we are not interested in that breed. We are interested in learning from those who have, by their examples, demonstrated a loyalty to noble principles. These people score high in the five disciplines of effectiveness. Their *nobility* of vision is seen in their quest for understanding, their independence, their purity of vision, their commitment to goodness, and their propensity for kindness.

People of true vision are also *revolutionary*. They pursue momentous and radical change. They take the road less traveled; they exhibit an uncommon loyalty to principles—even when surrounded by dissenters. These people abide by divine conscience, not public conscience. They are passionate about understanding and following their sacred, internal voice of wisdom. They become weary of the clamoring of public opinion. For example, they care less about the political correctness of lables (public conscience), and more about protecting the sanctity of the individual (divine conscience).

One Saturday I noticed a woman delivering our mail.

"Here comes the mail*man*," I said to my wife.

"You mean mail*person*," my wife said with a smile.

"I stand corrected," I said. I opened the front door just as the mail was being dropped into our mailbox and sang out, "Good morning, mail*person*." Then I smiled, expecting to be commended for my political savvy.

Instead, the woman shot me a dirty look and squawked, "I'm a letter carrier."

So be it.

People of true vision are champions of momentous and radical change when the status quo is in violation of truth. Perhaps that change is most dramatic when it is directed internally. The life of Oskar Schindler, as portrayed in Steven Spielberg's motion picture *Schindler's List*, demonstrates my point. Schindler was not a saint— he was a drinker, gambler, and womanizer who saw the exploitation of the Jews as an opportunity to become a millionaire. That is what makes his transformation so revolutionary, for he defrauded the Nazis for months by managing a munitions factory that never produced one usable shell. By war's end he was broke, but he had liberated over 1,000 Polish Jews.

I'm equally moved by common people who recognize the shame of their lives and take revolutionary action—momentous and radical—to change their state of being.

HISTORIC REVOLUTIONARY VISIONARIES

Think about some of the giants in history who have linked principles with revolutionary commitment:

- Herodotus (484 to 429 BC): To shift from the mythology of how things began to the consequences of history.
- Socrates (470 to 399 BC): To know right is to do right.
- Jesus Christ (1 BC to 29 AD): To love God and your neighbor as yourself.
- Thomas Aquinas (1225 to 1274): To recognize the complimentary nature of reason and faith.
- Nicolas Copernicus (1473 to 1543): To acknowledge the sun as center of the universe.
- Martin Luther (1483 to 1546): To receive salvation by faith alone and not by works.
- Galilei Galileo (1564 to 1642): To know that bodies do not fall with velocities proportional to their weights.
- René Descartes (1596 to 1650): To apply rational methods of science to philosophy.
- John Locke (1632 to 1704): To derive authority solely from the consent of the governed.
- Søren Kierkegaard (1813 to 1855): To recognize existence as a life of choice.
- Susan B. Anthony (1820 to 1906): To gain women's right to vote.
- Louis Pasteur (1822 to 1895): To prove the germ theory of disease.
- Marie Curie (1867 to 1934): To demonstrate that women can not only compete but excel in male-dominated professions.
- William James (1862 to 1910): To experience life as a fluid, dynamic "stream of consciousness."
- Mohandas K. Gandhi (1869 to 1948): To gain the independence of India through nonviolent civil disobedience.
- Orville (1871 to 1948) and Wilbur (1867 to 1912) Wright: To prove that man can fly.
- Albert Einstein (1879 to 1955): "To experience the universe as a single, significant whole."
- Igor Stravinsky (1882 to 1971): To explore all musical styles—including dissonance and shifting rhythms.

- Martha Graham (1893 to 1991): To dance with angularity and severity of movements.
- Rosa Parks (1913-): To challenge the constitutionality of segregation laws.

These people explored a myriad of disciplines. What they had in common was the revolutionary nature of their exploits. Although many were reviled by their contemporaries, they still clung to their vision. These were people of enormous courage, and, for that reason, their lives can be intimidating. Can we expect to match their commitment? Craig Keilburger did, and he was only 12 years old. Most revolutionaries are ordinary people with an extraordinary vision.

A REVOLUTIONARY MOTHER

Was my younger brother Ray in love with Sue Rutherford? I don't know. If looking dopey is being in love, Ray was shot through the heart. But at 13, it's hard to make those fine distinctions. For example, when is the right time to kiss a girl? Knowing when to kiss a girl is no simple matter. Ray decided to ask Sue's best friend, Angela.

"Are you sure?" Ray asked.

"Trust me," Angela said, "she really wants you to kiss her."

"But are you sure?"

"I'M SURE! And it has to be a long kiss."

A long kiss? What did that mean? Ray didn't know. So he turned to the one person in the world that he trusted, unconditionally—Mom.

"Mom, Angela says that Sue Rutherford reEEElly wants to kiss me. But it has to be a long kiss. So I want to kiss you, and you tell me if it's long enough. Okay?"

"Huh?" Mom said.

"Mom, are you listening?"

"Okay," she said, gathering her composure. "I'm Sue Rutherford, and you're going to kiss me."

"Yeah, but you have to tell me if it's long enough. That's the important part."

"Okay. I've got it."

With that, Ray gripped Mom's shoulders, puckered, and kissed her.

"How was that?"

"That, that was good," Mom said.

Ray was wondering if Mom was grasping the importance of this experiment. "But was it LONG enough?"

"That was definitely a long kiss. I would go with that."

The next day, after school, was the moment of truth. Ray was walking Sue home, carrying her books.

When they reached Sue's house, Ray decided to go for it.

"Okay, are you ready?" he asked, putting her books down and clutching both her shoulders, just as he had rehearsed with Mom.

"Uh huh."

Then he did it. He stepped forward and kissed her.

Ray was so happy he skipped all the way home.

Was the kiss long enough? Evidently not. The next day Angela told Ray that Sue was dumping him. Two days later, heartbroken, Ray saw Sue with Travis McKinsey, an athelete who was clearly more experienced in matters of the heart.

In time Ray recovered. The real winner in all this was Mom. She learned she had something precious: her son's unequivocal trust.

I call that revolutionary. When a mother is willing to put her lips on the line for her son's peace of mind, it is revolutionary. How often have we seen examples of mothers and fathers who do not have time for their children, who are not willing to engage their entire being in the parenting process? To break that mold, to embrace a child wholly, unequivocally, is as revolutionary as seeking out the mysteries of the universe.

So visions that are noble and revolutionary are not just for saints and Nobel Prize winners. They are for any one of us who is willing to stand up for truth.

A PERSONAL MISSION STATEMENT:
TO WRITE OR NOT TO WRITE

Do you have a mission statement? Have you composed a description of your highest ideals, your purpose in life?

Few people have written a personal mission statement, and many refuse to do it. I remember a conversation I had with a 50-year-old man. "I don't have to write a mission statement," he said. "I've always known where I'm going."

"Good," I said, "then you have nothing to lose."

"What do you mean?" he asked.

"If you've always known where you're going, writing a mission statement will be easy."

"Well, I'm still not doing it?"

I smiled. "Really? What are you afraid of? A man like you should be able to handle a little writing assignment."

Travis looked me straight in the eyes "Okay, if the truth be known, I don't know if I can keep my word."

"You could fail," I said, "and that's a hard pill to swallow. But an even harder pill to swallow is the pain of not trying."

Fear and laziness are the two most common reasons for not writing a mission statement. Fear is about what could happen (failure); laziness is about what might have to be accomplished (effort). Both fear and laziness are harbingers of personal discomfort; hence, they act as powerful deterrents. It is exceedingly easier to blame people or circumstances for our condition.

Why should you take on the challenge of writing a mission statement? Here are four compelling reasons.

1. To Create a Vision is Instinctual

Animals are blessed with a success instinct. Birds navigate great distances, sometimes over thousands of miles of open sea to return to their nesting grounds. Worker bees can navigate over a quarter of a mile from the hive in search of nourishing flowers; when they find their way back to the hive, they communicate the direction and distance to other bees though a twirling "dance." A newly hatched tortoise will immediately turn and head for the safety of the sea.

We human beings are also blessed with the instinct to create our own destiny. But, unlike the lower animals, we have the capacity, through imagination, to select our destiny. This cannot be avoided; people are creatures of vision. However, the latitude of human vision is enormous. Think of vision as a continuum. On one end is vision of inconsequence—mundane, perhaps even unprincipled; on the other end is vision: noble and revolutionary. Where we fall on the continuum is determined by the deliberateness of our efforts. I suggest that without a written declaration, we are more likely to select the commonplace: the next television soap opera; a mindless, internet chat room; or (a vision without action) simply the compulsion to get to the weekend.

2. To Create a Vision Is an Act of Independence.

We cannot avoid creating a vision. To live without vision is to live in pain; the human spirit will not tolerate it for long. Much of our language reflects our intolerance for life without vision. Without vision we feel the blahs, the blues, restless, cabin fever—"I'm bored." In addition, we rely on language to help us get the vision: what's the plan? what do we want to do now? how? when? where?

If we do not select our own vision, we will select a vision belonging to someone else. In 1963 a Yale University professor, Stanley Milgram, began a series of famous experiments. He recruited people to participate in a learning experiment. When the people arrived, a researcher (wearing a white lab coat and carrying a clipboard) greeted them. He explained that the experiment involved a "teacher" and a "learner." The learner was instructed to learn a list of word pairs. Later, the experimenter strapped the learner into a chair and attached an electrode to the learner's arm.

The teacher was placed in an adjourning room and instructed to read a list of word pairs to the learner, who repeated the list. If the learner did not respond accurately, the teacher was instructed to shock the learner, beginning with 15 volts of electricity and continuing, in 15-volt increments, to 450 volts.

Imagine that you are the teacher. What would you do? How much electricity would you inflict on the learner in the name of science? Most "teachers"—65 percent—chose to administer all 450 volts of electricity—to torture their "learners" through a strong compulsion to obey authority.

In a revised experiment, Milgram reversed the roles of the researcher and the "learner." The researcher instructed the teacher to stop delivering shocks, while the learner insisted that the experiment continue. In 100 percent of the cases, the teacher immediately followed the researcher's instructions to stop.

Obedience to figures of authority with ignoble, even evil, causes is not uncommon (Nazi death camps, Jones Town, and the My Lai massacre are three of the more terrifying examples). The danger is real. Therefore, if we are to obey any authority, does it not make sense to yield only to absolute principles, for if we abide by absolute truths (peace, love, forgiveness), making the right choice becomes clear. To create a vision for ourselves by writing a mission statement is equivalent to creating a personal guide of appropriate and ethical behavior.

To go against authority makes revolutionaries of us all. To do the right thing—despite the direction or advise from parents, teachers, peers, spouses, lawyers, or military officers—may result in disapproval, condemnation, attack, and even imprisonment and death. That is not uncommon ground for revolutionaries. Jesus Christ, Saint Paul, Gandhi, Martin Luther King, Nelson Mandela— all noble revolutionaries—endured man's inhumanity. But standing up for truth in the face of adversity is not restricted to world leaders; nor is it limited to earth-shattering causes. The common man or woman or the ordinary boy or girl who takes a stand on the little inequities in life is a revolutionist. The cause need not be cosmic in its scope; it need only be right.

Once I spoke at a conference on total quality. I proposed that a work group must first become a community before it can expect to achieve the status of a total quality organization.

Two days after the conference I received a call from Jill, a close friend of mine. Though the years we have enjoyed each other's company, particularly as tennis partners. It is the kind of relationship where we both can be irreverent without fear of judgment.

When Jill called that day, I could tell immediately from her voice that something was not right. She sounded like she was on the verge of tears.

"I'm not sure how to say this. It's something that concerns you and me, so I thought . . ."

"Boy, I sure hope somebody thinks we're having an affair," I said jokingly.

Jill paused for just an instant and then laughed. "Gee, you're sure taking this well."

"You mean it's true?"

"Yes," Jill said. "My neighbor was at the conference where you spoke the other day. Someone at her table said, 'Isn't that Allen Johnson, the guy who's having an affair with Jill?'"

"Life's too short to be bothered by such nonsense," I said. "Let them think what they want. But what about you? How are you feeling?"

"Well, I was angry at first and hurt too. It made me mad that someone would twist an innocent friendship into something lewd. But now, after talking to you, I feel okay."

I was glad that I was able to reframe the incident for Jill before she hardwired a negative memory. When she had called me, Jill was very vulnerable. My reaction had the capacity to either confuse or calm her. Naturally, I wanted her to relax, to release the emotional anger, physical tension, and the potential for future anxiety. I think I was successful.

The story of my "affair" with Jill is about being a revolutionary, to reject, even scorn, popular consensus when the populace is wrong. Jill and I did not let the incident ruin our friendship. Why should it? We are guided by the conviction that our character is not the byproduct of what other people think, but rather the consequence of our loyalty to the principles of discipline.

3. To Create a Vision Activates the Impulse for Personal Congruence.

I am blessed. I routinely speak to others about the joy of living a life founded on a vision of principles. Every time I share my vision, my commitment is reinforced. No one likes to be caught in a lie. We feel dissonance when what we say conflicts with our behavior (how we think, feel, and act). Lie detectors are based on that phenomena: we emit telltale electrical impulses when our words conflict with what we know to be the truth.

Social psychologists, Morton Deutsch and Harold Gerard, constructed an ingenious study that demonstrated the power of making public statements. In their study, college students were instructed to estimate the length of lines. They were separated into three groups. The first group was instructed to write down their estimates, sign, and relinquish the written estimates to the researcher. The second group was instructed to write their estimates on a Magic Writing Pad and then erase their estimates before anyone else saw them. The third group was instructed to only mentally record their estimates. Later, all three groups were given new evidence to suggest that their estimates were wrong and were then permitted to change their original estimates.

What Deutsch and Gerard learned was fascinating. The third group—the mental estimators—were most willing to change their original estimates. The second group—the private estimators—were significantly more loyal to their estimates. The first group—the public estimators—were clearly the most loyal to their original estimates.

The study demonstrates the influence of writing (even something as innocuous as an estimate of the length of lines), particularly when the writing is shared with others. If there was ever a study designed to show the benefits of writing a personal vision, it is this one. Simply the writing of words—not to mention the public announcement of those words—is enough to influence loyalty. So, take advantage of this absolutely free and powerful tool for enabling personal integrity.

4. To Create a Vision Internalizes a Belief System.

A close friend of mine once told me that he had a plan to lose 50 pounds.

"How will you do it?" I asked.

"My wife is going to do it for me," he said.

"Huh?"

"She is going to fix all my meals for me," he said, "to make certain that I eat the right kind and amount of food."

My friend's plan had failure written all over it. Indeed, the diet failed because it didn't belong to my friend—it belonged to his wife.

Enduring commitment must be owned by the individual. Commitment does not come from bribes or threats; it comes from an internal attachment to the belief.

A study by Jonathan Freedman provided strong evidence in support of this idea. Freedman wanted to know what it would take to prevent young boys from playing with an enticing mechanical toy robot. He set up two experimental groups. With the first group he told the boys, "It is wrong to play with the robot. If you play with the robot, I'll be very angry," Freedman then left the room for a few minutes and observed the boys. Only one of the 22 boys touched the robot. Six weeks later, the boys participated in a drawing test. At the conclusion of the test, the boys were told that they could play with any of five toys, including the coveted robot, while the researcher scored the tests. The other four toys (a plastic submarine, a toy rifle, a child's baseball glove, and a toy tractor) were far less intriguing, and so 17 of the boys chose to play with the robot—the toy that Freedman had forbidden six weeks earlier.

In the second group of boys, the procedure was identical to the first group, with this exception: Freedman only said to the boys, "It is wrong to play with the robot." No threat was issued. Again Freedman left the room, and, again, only one of the 22 boys chose to touch the robot. What was different occurred six-weeks later. This time when the researcher invited the boys to play with any of five toys, only seven of the boys chose the robot.

What made the difference? Although threats and bribes might instill commitment on the short-term—while an "enforcer" is present—it is much less likely to work on the long-term, when the enforcer is absent. Freedman suggested that the boys from the second group decided, for *intrinsic* reasons, that the robot was to be avoided; the idea was owned by them. It is that ownership that creates real commitment.

I experienced this principle when I was growing up. As a small boy, it was a special treat when my parents took my bother and me to the movies. But by the time I had turned nine, my mother began taking my brother and me to a Christian, fundamentalist church, where we were taught that going to movies was wrong. Neither my mother, nor the church, forbade me from seeing a movie—there was never the slightest threat—but I did stop. Now, I love movies, but for 10 years I never saw one. Why? I think the injunction was imprinted on my belief system. To my mind, my decision to avoid movies was not dictated by the church or my mother; it was dictated by my personal sense of what was right and wrong at the time.

Writing a personal mission statement is a painless way of internalizing high ideals. Once written, the statement—call it a personal constitution—becomes a template for the decisions of the day.

ABIDING BY A VISION: DO YOU OR DON'T YOU?

Creating a vision or personal mission should be taken seriously—not unlike a religious sacrament—for violating a vision disturbs the stability of personal serenity and interpersonal communion. Taking a mission statement lightly quickly stokes the fire of disillusionment.

Several years ago, I was in the market for a new car, a high-performance, luxury sedan. I did the research and chose a model that was at the top of the list in all categories—a prestigious automobile by anyone's standards. I located a dealership in Portland, Oregon and cut a deal over the phone. I purchased a one-way airline ticket to Portland, intending to drive my new car home.

When I walked into the showroom I was impressed with the glass walls and marble floors—a classy place. Then I saw the mission statement for the dealership. It was moving:

Three Rules We Live By.
Rule I—We will be loyal to our customers, honest with everyone, and unselfish in dealing with others.

Rule II—We won't accept anything less than the best we're capable of doing, and our customers have the right to expect the best that we can do for them.

Rule III—The only way to succeed in our relations with others is to have understanding, compassion, and trust for people.

After reading such inspiring words, I knew I was in good hands. I sat down in the salesman's cubicle, and we worked out the remaining details of the deal.

"Would you like to pick out a color?" the salesman said. "We have two units in stock to select from."

"You bet," I said beaming. I could hardly wait to get my hands on the wheel.

We walked out to the parking lot, and the salesman directed me to two glistening cars: One was gold-colored—a real beauty—the other a faded lavender.

"I'll take the gold one," I said with a smile.

"Not so fast," the salesman retorted. "It has a sunroof."

"I don't want a sunroof," I said.

"I know."

"So, how much is a sunroof?"

"$900," the salesman said.

"Well, I didn't want a sunroof, but . . . I'll take it."

"Not so fast," the salesman said. "The gold car is not just $900 more expensive than the lavender car; it's $2,900 more. You see, the gold car is equipped with the most popular accessories. And we know we can get that price."

Suddenly Rule I flashed before my eyes:

"We will be loyal to our customers, honest with everyone, and unselfish in dealing with others."

Don't give me that bunk about loyalty to customers, honesty, and unselfishness, I thought. This dealership's real mission should be, "Gouge the customer for whatever you can get."

Abiding by a mission is not something to fool with. Either you do or you don't. To have a mission and violate it is worse than having no mission at all. Why? Because you know better.

Now, I have a confession to make. Yes, I am driving the lavender car. At the time, I felt trapped: I was over 200 miles from home with no mode of transportation. Granted, it was probably a deal I should have walked away from. Three years later, I still feel a tinge of rancor whenever I slide behind the wheel—just one side-effect of a mission ignored.

WRITING A PERSONAL CONSTITUTION

The Constitution of the United States of America begins with a 52-word preamble:

We the people of the United States, in order to form a more perfect union, establish justice, insure domestic tranquility, provide the common defense, promote the general welfare, and secure the blessings of liberty to ourselves and our posterity, do ordain and establish this Constitution for the United States of America.

The preamble is followed by the seven articles. The first four delineate the powers attributed to congress, the president, the supreme court, and the states. That constitution—along with the 27 amendments, including the original Bill of Rights (the first 10 amendments)—superceded the Articles of Confederation in 1789 and has kept the United States on a course of democracy.

Our constitution is a vision of substance. The preamble offers a core of nobility for the nation: justice, tranquility, common defense, general welfare, and the blessings of liberty. The seven articles and the amendments to follow establish a revolutionary design; the constitution broke the tradition of English monarchy and established, once and for all, a sovereign democracy.

A personal constitution should also fulfill these requirements: a statement of nobility and a statement of revolution.

A Personal Constitution	
Preamble	Articles
Core of nobility	Revolutionary design
The why	The who, how, and what
The ideology	The purpose
The principles	The function
The character	The behavior
The spiritual inheritance	The calling

The preamble to a personal constitution captures your core of nobility, your highest ideals. If you are not sure what that is, ask yourself, "What qualities—what ways of being—do I hold most dear?" Then ask yourself why. Then ask why again. You will get to the core in no time. It is a question I cherish asking; when people put into words the qualities that they value most, their eyes shine with emotion.

"What qualities—what ways of being—do you hold most dear?" I will ask.

"Honor."

"Why honor?"

"Because my word is my bond?"

"But why?"

"Because my life is not worth living otherwise. If the people I care about—my wife, my children, my co-workers—can't depend on me, I may as well cash it in."

"Why would you do that?" I ask.

"Because without honor you are not making a contribution. You are not providing leadership, you are not offering an example that others can follow, you are not leaving the world in a better place."

At this point I see the flush of the skin, the tremble in the mouth, the tears in the eyes, and I know that I have reached the core. All I can do is nod and say, "I see."

Why do I do what I do? For the nation, the answer is found in the preamble of the constitution. For the person I interviewed, the answer is found in words laced with emotion: for honor, for making a contribution, for leaving the world in a better place. That is the start of a strong preamble to a personal constitution. There is probably more. I would follow-up with another question: "What other qualities do you hold most dear?" They might talk about tolerance, patience, forgiveness, service; whatever they say will form the foundation of their preamble.

I call the preamble a spiritual inheritance. We are born with a foundation of absolute truths in place. The preamble to our personal constitution is an articulation of that inheritance. Be silent for a moment and you will hear it.

The Articles of a Personal Mission Statement: A Revolutionary Design

The articles of a personal mission statement (like the articles of the United States constitution) capture the responsibilities of predominate roles. Your roles are unlikely to be legislative, executive, and judicial, but they are likely to be spouse, friend, and employee. In your articles you will detail your function. I call it a *calling*, for personal roles are as much a gift as they are a selection. Some are called to parenthood—they have the sense that being a mother or a father is their ultimate mission or purpose in life. Others are called to roles of leadership, others to roles of service, still others to roles of creative expression. The articles of a mission statement clarify these roles and the ideal behaviors they are to project.

To develop the articles of your mission statement, respond to the following six instructions:

1. Select a key role—son/daughter, mother/father, friend, employee, manager, artist, community leader, volunteer, self. (The *who* you are.)

2. List your unique, positive qualities related to the selected role. (That is *what* you have to give.)
3. Write down how you enjoy expressing these qualities. (That is *how* you can give.)
4. Describe the perfect world as it relates to the selected role. (That is a description of your ideal state.)
5. Write an article for the role selected by drawing on your unique, positive qualities (step 2) and the manner of expressing those qualities (step 3) for the purpose of closing the gap between where you are now and where you would like to be (step 4).
6. Repeat steps 2 through 5 for each major role.

Here's how an article of a personal mission might emerge for the role of manager.

1. Role: Manager
2. My unique, positive qualities:
   • Friendly, caring attitude
   • Good listening skills
   • Able to give directions clearly
   • Solid grasp of technical requirements
   • Understanding of the political culture
   • Solve problems and resolve conflict
   • Able to think systemically
   • Customer orientation

3. How I enjoy expressing my qualities:
   • Coaching and mentoring
   • Counseling
   • Teaching
   • Strategic planning
   • Excellent customer service

4. The perfect world:
   - We whole-heartedly support the development of our employees.
   - Our department is a hotbed of creativity and innovation.
   - We solve problems the right way—getting to the root, not just the symptom, of the problem.
   - Our employees are experts—stars in their field.
   - We help make the company more profitable by offering services that satisfy all the customer's needs—even the unspoken needs.
   - It is a fun place to work.
   - We work as a team, continually soliciting the ideas of all team members—even ideas that seem off the wall.
   - Our customers love us.

5. An article of my personal mission statement:
   Role: Manager

   I am a builder of people, able to provide a nurturing environment that supports and, when necessary, transforms every employee into a company star. I teach my associates to see the big picture, to consider all angles when solving problems posed by internal and external customers.

   I believe in teams. I build team spirit by valuing the contribution of all members. We have fun creating new ideas. I mentor and coach those who feel shy about expressing their ideas.

   Our customers are analyzed holistically. The team considers and addresses all dimensions of the customer—financial, interpersonal, even spiritual. We are fast, friendly, and flexible with our customers.

Notice how each step of developing a personal mission article builds on the previous step. For example, the unique quality of good listening supports the expression of mentoring and counseling. In turn, mentoring and counseling support the ideal state of an environment that nurtures employee development and creativity. Steps 2 through 4 support the emergence of the article itself.

MY PERSONAL MISSION STATEMENT

I would like to share my personal mission statement with you—not because it is the definitive personal constitution, but because it may serve as a modest source of inspiration. The statement has been subdivided to facilitate the commentary that follows each section.

Mission preamble

I am a positive and tranquil adult, secure in my self-image and at peace with myself. I have nothing to prove to others and everything to prove to myself. When I have a choice between being right and being kind, I chose to be kind. I am liberated of vanity.

I have nothing to prove to others when I am living by principles. This is liberating. I don't have to prove to anyone how nifty I am. Whew! It's nice to be out of that business.

I live a life of dignity and integrity—regardless of the circumstances—striving always to achieve self-actualization for myself while encouraging the discovery of personal truth for others. I respond to challenges in the spirit of joy and adventure.

Living a life of dignity and integrity—regardless of the circumstances—is one of my most deep-seated beliefs.

The last sentence is a direct quote from my wife. I admit that there are some household jobs that get under my skin, and I sometimes choose to behave irascibly. Plumbing is one such task; I abhor everything about it: bruised knuckles, hair balls, and tight spaces. One Saturday morning I decided to tackle a drip under the kitchen sink. I asked my wife if she would help me. "Sure, Honey," she said, "but could we do this in the spirit of joy and adventure?" That same day I added my wife's words to my personal mission.

I believe in leaving a legacy. That which is not given is lost.

What opportunities for kindness have we passed up by hoarding our talent, knowledge, and resources? Sharing what we have is good for three reasons: good for the receiver, good for the giver, and good for the community. When we turn down opportunities to share our gifts with others, we are the losers.

When we step into an elevator, we quickly push the buttons for our floor. What if we used that opportunity for kindness? When someone joins me in an elevator, I now ask, "What floor, please?" When I enter an elevator that is already occupied, I ask the other person to push the button for my floor. That little exchange is a gift for both of us.

Mission articles

Husband. *I am loving and attentive to my wife. I nurture and support her in all things. I constantly seek to affirm her. I make at least one date with her each week. I cherish her uniqueness. I strive to understand and be sensitive to her needs and aspirations.*

Do you think my wife likes that? Sometimes my wife talks about things at the end of the day that are marginally interesting to me—test scores for second graders, for example. And sometimes my wife will take detours, beginning with a discussion of teaching methods and ending, somehow, with an impassioned soliloquy on a hybrid sunflower. Still, our relationship is healthier when I stay plugged in.

One date a week nourishes our partnership. We are independent—Nita and I—and if we were not to make an effort, we could someday find ourselves living separate lives in the same house. For us, that's not a marriage; it's an arrangement.

Family member. *I have a genuine interest in the lives of my family. I am always available when called on. I am a loving and supportive son and brother. I am trusted; I never engage in confessing their sins.*

Being available when called on is important to me. I sometimes feel a tinge of disappointment if a family member is unavailable to me. Although it's usually unavoidable and understandable, it can still sting a little. Knowing how that can feel, I try to be there when my company is solicited. Here's an example.

I had my Saturday all planned. I was going to get up early and exercise: a three-mile run and 20 minutes of stretching. Then I planned to put in an hour at the piano, followed by several hours at the computer writing. After lunch I would mow the lawn, wash the car, and try to make some sense out of the garage. These are all worthy pursuits, but when measured against the vital, they don't carry much weight.

Early that morning, my brother Ray called. "Hey, Al," he said, "you wanna go play?"

I thought about two seconds and said, "You bet."

Ray was over to my house in 15 minutes. We jumped in his car and drove down to the park where we played one-on-one basketball, just as we did when we were kids. Later we had lunch and went to a movie.

Was it the right thing to do? No question for me. It's part of being a loving and supportive brother. To pass an opportunity to spend a Saturday in fellowship with my brother, particularly when measured against trivial pursuits, would be a violation of my mission.

Friend. I take time to develop and nurture friendships. I respond immediately and cheerfully to a call for aid. I share myself and my resources with my friends; I have an abundance mentality. I do not engage in one-upsmanship. I seek to understand and respect the diversity of others. I offer advice only when advice is solicited.

Try not offering advice until it is solicited—it is tough! My tendency is to sprinkle others with my "unfathomable" wisdom. For years I failed to notice that most people simply brushed it aside.

Learner. I am always expanding my knowledge and my experience. I am always seeking and having new adventures. I am humble as a learner.

My role as a learner is the crux of my joy in life. I love the beginnings: the excitement that grows out of a new experience. I tend to be experiential in all aspects of my life: my teaching, conversations, hobbies, and special interests. I don't want to lecture about an idea; I want to demonstrate it, get immersed in it. I don't want to talk about the weather; I want to talk about dreams, ambitions, relationships. I don't want to read about scuba diving or mountain climbing or playing jazz; I want to do it. I want to dive in tropical waters where the life is abundant, the colors vibrant, and the visibility endless. I want to figure out a way to traverse a glacier crevasse. I want to feel the exhilaration of playing off the ideas of other musicians when the band is hot and the audience is on the edge of their seats. That's what I love: the experience.

Teacher, mentor, change agent. I believe in sharing knowledge; I share the best information I have. I seek opportunities to help others realize their dreams. I celebrate with those who are growing. I have a thorough understanding of the art and craft of helping individuals and groups make positive change. I select and employ the most elegant tool for the situation. My character models the changes I recommend.

I get a kick out of watching people grow. It's the little steps that tickle me. I have a friend who recently realized that he doesn't have to be a bully at work to get the job done, that, in fact, he is more likely to accomplish tasks on time with a good dose of kindness and tolerance. That new awareness is a delight to see.

In business I want to get executives on the fast track to growth. That requires a thorough knowledge of a myriad of leadership and organization development tools. Selecting just the right tool at the right time can move a manager to the next level of effectiveness.

Am I there? No. Am I getting better? Yes. I am convinced that the longer I live with my mission—the more I remain loyal to its creed—the closer I will align with it. That's the joy of growing up.

A personal constitution is like a navigational gyroscope. At the core is the axis: a straight and true pin, without which the device would be useless. Around the axis is the flywheel—continually spinning around the axis.

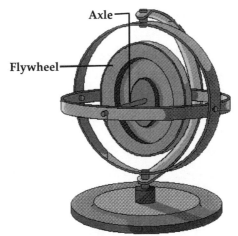

Think of the axis as the mission preamble—your spiritual inheritance. It must be straight and true, for everything else spins around it. The flywheel is akin to the mission articles. It is continually spinning—a whirling dervish of activities as spouse, family member, friend, employee, volunteer. The flywheel (with all its ebullient roles) will wobble, falter, even stop functioning altogether, without a core axis of structural integrity.

THE LANGUAGE OF VISION

How would you recognize a person of vision? One clue is to listen to their words. Language is the outward manifestation of our inner thoughts. What we say—whether inspiring or frivolous—represents the stature of our vision.

- I have a dream.
- I have this picture in my head.

- I woke up this morning with an insight (or solution to my problem).
- I am driven by this extraordinary vision.
- I have a personal mission (or calling).
- I have this hunch. I want to check it out to see if it is real. If it is I may consider incorporating it into my belief system.
- What would happen if we did this?
- What do you want to accomplish?
- What do you want to become?
- Imagine a perfect world. What would be your role in it?
- What is the right thing to do?
- I have a responsibility to do the right thing.
- How can I change for the better?
- I remain true to my mission.
- Let's see if we can find a better way.

THE ACTIVITIES OF VISION

Of course, the real value of the vision is not what we say, but what we do. How do people of vision behave? What action do they take when all is right with the world? What do they do in moments of crisis?

- I write a personal constitution.
- I consult my mission when making decisions.
- Before starting a task, I visualize the completed product or service.
- Before saying or doing something risky, I consider the impact my words or actions will have on other people.
- I make plans for the week.
- I make plans for the future.
- I save for what I want.
- I apologize when I have violated my mission.
- I make decisions and take action based on my highest ideals, not based on the potential for praise or extrinsic rewards.
- I picture myself being successful.

PUTTING VISION TO WORK

We've talked a great deal about creating a vision for ourselves. Here is a way of helping others to discover for themselves a personal work-related vision. The following four items can be posed to one individual or to team members who are working on the same assignment:

1. Name an important project that you care about. [This statement specifies a key article of the mission.]
2. Why do you care about the project? [This question gets to the principles encompassed in a constitution preamble.]
3. Ideally, how would you like the project to be in three years? [This question helps to create a perfect vision for the task. Responses that reflect a belief system contribute to the preamble; responses that address behaviors contribute to the mission articles.]
4 Ideally, throughout the accomplishment of this task, how would you like employees of this company to treat the internal and external customers? [This question returns to a constitution article: how to treat a customer.]

Using these four items as a template, a manager can now lead a discussion to help people clarify their role and purpose.

"Sam, I'd like to see if we can clarify how you see your role within our group."

"What's one important project that you really care about?"

"Well, for me it's marketing the new X9-1000."

"Why do you care so much about that project?"

"Because it could be a huge source of revenue for the company, and it would boost the reputation of our department."

"What do you mean by that?" the manager presses.

"If we can make the X9-1000 a big hit, we can write our ticket for other projects. We will have the reputation for being the go-to guys—the team that markets the virtues of any project with integrity."

"Why is integrity so important to you?"

"If we're true to the product and the customer, everyone wins. The best way to gain customer loyalty is to give them a product that they can trust."

"Suppose that three years down the road the X9-1000 is a blockbuster. What would that look like?"

"Well," Sam says, "customers would be knocking our door down. People would feel they can't live without our product. They would praise its friendliness and reliability. They would come to us with new spin-off ideas for the X9-1000. And we would respond with speed and agility—working with them to enhance the product and create new products."

The manager is furiously taking notes. "This is great," he says. "As we move ahead on this project, how would we treat our internal and external customers?"

"We would treat them with integrity. We would listen. We would get to the root of what our customers need."

Soon the manager and Sam have more than enough material to put together a statement of vision.

A Vision for the X9-1000 Project

Mission preamble

Integrity is our most treasured principle. We believe in being true to our products and to the customers we serve. We know that our reputation hinges on it. We also recognize that integrity ultimately converts into customer loyalty and increased revenue.

Mission articles

Customer service. *We honor our customers by listening to them wholeheartedly. We get to the root of what they need. We treat them with the utmost integrity.*

The department. *We're the go-to guys. The company feels confident in coming to us with any marketing assignment. We are known for our stance on marketing with integrity.*

Innovation. *We work with our customers to enhance and create new products that serve the special needs of our customers.*

Sam (and his manager) now have something to turn to when trying to decide the right course of action. This concise vision statement didn't take long to develop, but, simple as it is, it provides Sam with a navigational gyroscope and instills motivation. The best part is it all came from within Sam, the only place where lasting motivation can emerge.

Chapter 8

THE DISCIPLINE OF COMMITMENT

THE PATH OF TRUTH AND IMPORTANCE

I do not know what I may appear to the world; but to myself I seem to have been only like a boy playing on the sea-shore, and diverting myself in now and then finding a smoother pebble or a prettier shell than ordinary, whilst the great ocean of truth lay all undiscovered before me.

—Isaac Newton

Lew Zirkle is an orthopedic surgeon in the city where I live. He is 59 years old but looks 10 years younger. He does not drive a Mercedes, and he never wears a watch; I don't think he owns a suit. He is the only M.D. I know who runs 4.5 miles to work in the morning and bicycles 4.5 miles home at the end of the day. He is a masterful surgeon and one of the most compassionate persons I've ever met.

Lew was raised on a small goat farm in Berkshire County, Massachusetts. From the beginning, he had his chores. It was his job to milk the goats and feed the rabbits, chickens, and pigs. If he didn't do it, it didn't get done.

"That was the way my father helped me develop my sense of worth," Lew told me one day. "He gave me a place that was essential to the welfare of the family."

How important, I thought, to cultivate that sense of responsibility in children.

"Dad was my friend," Lew continued. "I worked with him every day after school and on weekends. I liked that. Sometimes he depended on me to mend a fence in a tight spot where only I could reach. Plus he was always there when I needed him. He had a quiet way of letting me know that he cared—like resting his hand on my shoulder while I worked."

The values that Lew learned from his father set the foundation for an outstanding professional career. Lew won a football scholarship to Davidson University in North Carolina. At that time he had no burning desire to be a physician; he started taking pre-med courses because his friends in the dorm were doing it.

After Davidson, Lew was accepted into Duke University Medical School. He loved it. The professors were topnotch and the patients were unforgettable. With every new year his passion for medicine grew.

While in residency he was drafted into the army. The year was 1968, and Lew was sent to Vietnam.

"What was that like?" I asked.

"I worked in an evacuation hospital in the hottest sector of the country," he said. "I operated on one man after another. Through it all I felt a deep anger for senseless human suffering. I began to understand the meaning of the expression 'the family of man.'"

Lew's skill as a surgeon was soon recognized by the hospital staff. When General Westmoreland praised his work, Lew said, "I was untouchable. With the General's backing, I could do anything. I started treating Vietnamese civilians as well as our soldiers."

"It sounds like your social conscience matured in those months," I said.

"Maybe. What is a social conscience anyway? Just the realization that except for an accident of birth I could be that less fortunate human being."

That compassion for all people continues to be a basic tenet of Lew's value system. Today he is the program chairman for Orthopedics Overseas in Vietnam. In that capacity he volunteers two to four weeks of his time each year to train native physicians in the most advanced surgical techniques. That work has taken him (at his own expense) to Vietnam, Indonesia, Thailand, Ecuador, and Peru.

At home, Lew established a drug rehabilitation center for our community. Lew was on the streets counseling and treating hard-core addicts. ("We were not very successful," Lew admits. "The project only lasted a year.")

More recently Lew has created a nonprofit, international organization called Surgical Implant Generation Network (SIGN). "Open fractures are on the increase in developing countries by 17 percent," Lew explained. "Motorcycles are a common form of transportation in these countries—and the most deadly. Many patients are untreated or treated with outdated methods. I have seen patients bedridden for two to three years. That's where SIGN comes in."

I could hear the excitement in Lew's voice as he explained the concept.

"I want to do three things," Lew said. "One, I want to teach physicians in developing countries the proper protocol for treating fractures; supply the implant hardware—the rods, plates, and screws; and follow the physicians' progress over 30 implants and help them to manufacture their own surgical implants. I want them to take control of their own practices, to create self-sustaining teaching centers—but first they have to be properly trained."

"Where will the money come from?" I asked.

"My pocket," Lew said. "And from Dad," he added.

Having heard Lew's tribute to his father, I could understand why Lew's dad would want to help his son finance the project.

Although he gives much to his community and profession, Lew still makes time for family. He has been married for 35 years. His wife Sara is a pediatrician. He has three daughters, all graduates from Duke University. The oldest is a lawyer, on staff at

Georgetown University, specializing in mediation. The second daughter went on to Yale Medical School where she graduated first in her class; she is now doing her residency at Harvard in head and neck surgery. Lew's youngest daughter inherited her father's passion for public health in third-world countries and decided to work in India. She is now at Emory University.

"You raised a terrific family. How did you do it?" I asked.

"Sara and I always made time for our family," he told me. "When our daughters were at home, we were always available. If they wanted to talk, I dropped what I was doing. If it meant studying a little later into the night, that was fine. As for my wife and me, we reserve a quite time from 10 to 10:30 every night. We sit on a couch in the family room and talk."

I have always admired Lew—I feel at peace in his company. He has discovered the true meaning and importance of family. Lew knows that all people—from the partner at his side, to the patient 6,000 miles away in Vietnam—respond to the human touch.

• • •

People with a healthy and vital sense of commitment are voracious learners, constantly seeking to expand personal knowledge and experience, and stalwart and active defenders of their important relationships.

EXPANDING OUR KNOWLEDGE BASE

Before 1977, life was divided into two domains of life: *bacteria* (simple life-forms with cells that usually lack a nucleus) and *eucarya* (complex organisms—animals, plants, fungi—with cells that usually have a nucleus). All that changed with the research of Carl Woese, a microbiologist at the University of Illinois. He showed that there was a genetically distinct third type of life—possibly the most common organism on earth—that he called *archaea*. Archaea survives in the most hostile environments (in deep-sea thermal vents or in hypersaline water), but is also abundant in the plankton of open seas. Although scientists suggest that archaea is the most primitive organism on earth, it was only recently discovered. This biology lesson is a reminder to me to be humble as a learner; we simply do not know it all. Our understanding of truth is, at best, limited. Although our views of the world are sometimes wrong, more often than not, they are simply incomplete.

SEEKERS OF TRUTH AND PRISONERS OF FALSEHOOD

People who exercise the discipline of commitment have an unquenchable thirst for truth. They delight in it. They seek it for themselves and encourage it in others. They would rather endure the pangs of what can be unsettling truth than acquiesce to the tyranny of posturing, condescension, or Machiavellian deceit.

Disciples of commitment may also be recognized for what they are not. The table below contrasts seekers of truth with prisoners of falsehood.

Seekers of truth	Prisoners of falsehood
Citizens of open-mindedness	Captives of close-mindedness
Patrons of diversity	Patrons of prejudice
Defenders of understanding	Accomplices of stereotyping
Advocates of curiosity	Victims of fear
Guardians of democracy	Guardians of monarchy

I will explore each characteristic of the seekers of truth.

Citizens of Open-Mindedness

Citizens of open-mindedness are liberated. They are not restricted by conventional wisdom. That is not to say that they discount it (for, indeed, convention may be grounded in truth)—only that they are not limited by it. In fact, if you would like to see disciples of truth stiffen their resolve, suggest that they be a little more conventional.

Case in point: Cliff Young. Ultramarathons are organized footraces that extend far beyond the standard 26-mile marathon. There are 50-milers, 100-milers, even 1,000-milers. In fact, the longest certified ultramarathon in the world is New York's Sri Chinmoy—The Ultimate Ultra—that is run on a one-mile loop that runners circle 1,300 times. But if that is not enough of a challenge, you might consider the New York to Los Angeles Trans American

Footrace: a 64-day race that covers nearly 3,000 miles at approximately 45 miles a day. At the end of two months, you know you have accomplished something.

Cliff Young is an ultramarathoner. He entered the world of ultrarunning in 1983 when he won the 875-kilometer (544-mile) Sydney to Melbourne race—leaving the legendary ultrarunners of the day in his dust. Cliff's winning time—blitzing the course record by nearly two days—was five days, 15 hours, and four minutes. Oh, one other thing: In 1983 Cliff Young was 61 years old.

Cliff Young's profile did not match the typical long-distance runner. He was an Australian potato farmer who worked out by rounding up his cows on foot. He showed up at the Sydney to Melbourne race in bib overalls and galoshes. The wiry, old man offered an amusing spectacle.

Cliff was not restrained by what the "experts" had to say about ultramarathon running strategy. After all, conventional wisdom said that runners must sleep at least six hours out of every 24; Cliff slept only 11 hours in five-plus days. He didn't know about fancy running shoes or complicated diets; he just ran—and became a national hero in the process.

As of this writing, Cliff Young is 75 years old and planning to circumvent Australia—a 9,942 mile leg-stretcher. His plan is to take eight to nine months, covering 40 to 47 miles a day. His reason for running around Australia? To raise money for street kids.

Cliff is, indeed, a citizen of open-mindedness. He is creating his own truth—truth without limits. In 1987 I corresponded with Cliff's wife, Mary Young, who said this of her husband: "He is always saying he won't let things beat him! Although he has mellowed a little, he is still pretty stubborn!" People of commitment do have a certain tenacity about them. They are a little annoyed by the so-called pundits of the world who label reality. It makes them bristle, for no single person is the guardian of truth.

Patrons of Diversity

Seekers of truth are committed to celebrating diversity. I like to use the metaphor of a Greek wedding celebration. Recently, my cousin, Elaine, was married. Her father and mother—Uncle John and Aunt Soitera—are 100 percent Greek and know how to throw a party. After a beautiful ceremony in an awe-inspiring Greek Orthodox church, all the wedding guests retreated to a hotel for dinner, toasts, singing, dancing, laughter, and a whole lot of hugging.

I have never been able to get the hang of those tricky, Greek dance steps, but I danced the night away trying.

A wedding celebration marks the passage of two people becoming one. It's not a time for casual approval (certainly not a time for past resentments), but rather a time for unbridled rejoicing. A patron of diversity lifts his glass to all toasts for all parties; he dances with all revelers: the young, the old, the skinny, the chubby. A patron of diversity does not judge his dance partner; he simply dances with unrestrained exultation. To celebrate diversity is to live life like a Greek wedding.

The older I get, the more I relish a new take on life. Once every few months I like to have a jazz jam session at my home. I invite the neighbors and a half-dozen musician friends. We always rattle the rafters with enthusiastic riffs and rhythms.

At one of these sessions, I invited a friend who sang first soprano with a black gospel group called the Anointed. She showed up with the entire group. For an hour, they rocked the house with soulful gospel. A few weeks later, the group invited me to sing with them one Sunday evening in their home, the Morning Star Baptist Church.

The service was to begin at 7 p.m. I was there at 6:30. That was a mistake; the doors were locked. When a tall, lean black man unlocked the door at 6:55, I wondered if I had the right church.

"Excuse me, does the service start at 7 p.m.?" I asked.

"Sure 'nuff," said the man with a broad smile.

I walked into the small cinder block church and sat down on the front pew and waited. At about 7:15 the congregation began to drift in. At 7:30 the service began.

Being the only white face in an all-black congregation, I knew I was in for a cultural experience. The opening prayer set the tone. The tall man who had opened the door for me was the preacher. He stepped to the pulpit and smiled at the congregation. "Let us pray," he said.

"Oh, Lord," the preacher began, "we sing your praise. We raaaaise your name to the sky. God of Abraham, Lord of Hosts, Almighty Father—ga-lory to your name." The words rolled out into the congregation with grace and ease. The people accented each phrase with words of praise and encouragement.

"Hallelujah."

"Amen."

"Glory be to God."

At the same time the piano player backed up the preacher like a sax player fills in the phrases for a jazz singer.

Preacher: They shall mount up with wings as eagles.

Piano player: Mount up, mount up, Lord.

Preacher: They shall run and not be weary.

Piano player: Wearrrr-y. Ain't weary now.

Preacher: They shall walk and not faint.

Piano player: No time to faint, Lord, no time to faint.

It was all improvised, pure jazz. When it was my turn to sing, I was feeling the Spirit.

"We're proud to have a special guest join us today," the preacher said. "Come on up here, brother Allen."

As I stepped to the front of the church, I was jolted by a surge of emotion that straightened my spine. A cascade of benedictions burst from the congregation.

"Amen."

"Praise the Lord."

I was numbed by their gift of unconditional love.

"I've never had a welcome quite like that before," I said.

"Bless you, Son."

"Amen, brother."

"I know there are days when times seem rough," I said.

"Yes, they do."

"I know there are times when the day is long."

"Yes."

Suddenly I realized that it was happening to me. I was improvising with the audience, or the audience with me.

"But when the day is tough . . ."

"Yes, Lord."

". . . and the road is long . . ."

"My Lord."

"Amazing grace will see us through."

With that the Anointed sang the opening chord to Amazing Grace. I opened my mouth to sing. "Amazing grace, how sweet the sound . . ."

The Anointed began to clap on the offbeats. The congregation joined in, standing. I found myself in dialogue with the congregation.

"When we've been there 10,000 years . . ."

"Sing the song."

". . . bright shining as the sun . . ."

"Hallelujah, praise be to God."

And when the last chord was played, the congregation applauded—many of them with their hands high over the heads.

At that moment I was as happy as I have ever been. The joy of preacher, piano player, singers, congregation—and God— coming together in one magical moment of harmony and praise was, for me, fellowship of inconceivable richness. I tell you, I felt so jubilant, I was ready to climb Jacob's ladder to heaven's gate. What amazes me is this: until that moment, such coming together had been hidden from me. Is it worth celebrating? Amen, brother.

Defenders of Understanding

The Danish philosopher, Søren Kierkegaard, once said that when we label others, we negate them. There is great wisdom in that observation. We so want to categorize and catalogue others; it makes everything so neat and tidy, for as soon as I label you, I no longer have to think about you—I no longer have to seek to understand. How convenient.

Convenient, maybe, but also sad, for when I fail to go beyond the surface—when I treat another human being not as a person, but as an object—I risk overlooking a new idea, a novel experience, or a heart of gold.

This is the true account of how I kissed the neck of a liberated woman and lived to tell the story.

Rebecca (not her real name) called herself a modern woman. She believed in equal rights for all people, but especially for women. Although married, she vowed from the beginning that she would never become an object of domestic servitude. That's fair enough; to treat another like a second-class citizen is never just. Still, I have to admit that I was put off by Rebecca's style. Maybe it was her refusal to shave her legs and arm pits ("A vestige of men's warped fantasies of women as sex-kittens," she said). Maybe it was her insistence to retain separate and equal laundry days: her husband did his wash on Wednesday; Rebecca did her wash on Thursday. She seemed perpetually angry.

I met Rebecca in Algeria. Like myself, she and her husband were teaching English in a mountain Berber village. We did not hit it off. Candidly, in those days, if I had met her in the States, I would have dismissed her outright.

But I was not in the States. I was more or less forced to be with Rebecca; Rebecca and her husband were the only game in town. We had other friends—the Algerians and the French—but after a while, you long to speak in your own language; you'd like to talk about baseball or Snicker bars or drive-in theaters and know you're being understood.

So, reluctantly, my wife and I spent a lot of time with Rebecca. We celebrated all the American holidays together. And on the weekends we piled into our encrusted VW bug, drove to the Mediterranean, and camped on the beach.

Then a funny thing happened. Slowly, I began to see Rebecca as a person. I learned about her Mid-west upbringing, her favorite books (anything by D. H. Lawrence), and her greatest fears (to go unnoticed). I came to understand her better. I learned that she was vulnerable, compassionate, disciplined, and funny. I came to love her—hairy legs and all.

When I reached that place of acceptance, Rebecca and I became friends. Our relationship was protected by an envelope of understanding and mutual respect.

When my wife and I left Algeria, it was hard to say goodbye to Rebecca. I took her into my arms and held her a long time. Then I tried to to kiss her on the cheek, but at that instant she shifted her head, and my lips somehow landed on the nape of her neck.

"What's that about?" she asked with a giggle.

"I-I-I don't know," I said. "It must be your perfume."

Rebecca came back with: "Yeah, right, that would be Sweat by Faberge."

That was how I kissed the neck of a liberated woman and lived to tell the story.

Some 20 years later I looked Rebecca up in the States. She was a professor at a southwestern university, a Ph.D. in communications, specializing in cross-cultural understanding. She was teaching what she had taught me: tolerance.

Being a defender of understanding requires discipline. It means treating the other as a person—not an object. Here is the difference between a person and an object:

An object	A person
Measurable	Unbounded
Replicable	Unique
Mindless	Reflective

As soon as I have labeled someone ("oh, she's just a women's libber, like all the others"), I have turned a human being into an object. That is wrong. That is why I don't care very much for psychological instruments that pin a tag on the respondent or the people the respondent knows. Although they're enormously popular and scientifically reliable, I question the ultimate value of assessments like the Myers-Briggs Type Indicator. If used offhandedly, such instruments can convert people into measurable, replicable, mindless objects. Such instruments aim to distinguish how we are different. Of course, we are different (more different than any instrument can define), but vastly more important is how we are the same: how we share the same human spark, the same irrevocable ancestry of principles, and the same five human competencies.

The more I got to know Rebecca, the more I came to understand how we were more alike than different: both of us vulnerable, ambitious, wanting to love and be loved. If we are to disengage from treating free spirits like so much personal property, we must learn that to know you is to know me.

Advocates of Curiosity

I could see the top; it was, maybe, 50 yards away. But my legs would not move. Every muscle and bone in my body was screaming: "Sit Down!"

That was at 12,000 feet, approaching the summit of Mount Adams in Southern Washington. My partner, Paul, and I had been climbing for 10 hours. In that time we had ascended nearly 7,000 feet in elevation.

The first leg, to the timber line, was easy. Then the trail turned to shale on the dormant volcano. I studied every step, testing for solid footing on the igneous rock.

After that, we hit the snow fields. We broke out our ski poles and propelled ourselves forward—step-pull, step-pull. I was thinking, this mountain climbing isn't that tough. Sure, my backpack was wearing and my feet were sore, but I wasn't winded—not yet.

That was at 10,000 feet; from that point on the air was thinner. We stopped for a long drink of water and a handful of dried fruit.

I looked up the south side of the mountain: a massive glacier glaring in the sun. The false summit, at 11,500 feet, loomed overhead. The true summit was hidden from view some 800 feet in elevation beyond.

The trail to the false summit was steep. It was time to strap on our crampons—metal spikes, over an inch long. I replaced my ski poles with an ice ax.

I know, now, why they call the ascent to the top of a mountain an *assault*; it is murderous. For the last 2,000 feet of elevation, I began to mentally drift. How good it would be, I thought, to take off my pack, lie down, and sleep.

"Get hold of yourself," I said out loud. "You go to sleep on this mountain, and you might not wake up again." I began counting my strides. On the last 1,000 feet, every step was a step of will. After four small paces, I stopped, one foot ahead of the other, and breathed deeply. I averaged maybe 15 steps every minute. At that point everything was an annoyance. My collar bone and hip pointers ached from the pack, my calves were starting to cramp, and a mix of sweat and sun block lotion blurred my vision.

About 50 yards from the top, my body was ready to quit. But looking up, I saw Paul standing at the summit, his arms over his head in triumph.

I took another step forward. My boot broke through the snow and plunged down to above my knee. It took all my remaining strength to pull myself erect. I was breathing much harder now. I chose my steps more carefully—one step after another—in one last, slow march to the summit.

At the top, the world was mine. I could see it all: Mount Rainier to the north, Mount Hood to the south, and the gray, headless Mount St. Helens to the west. All at once I felt both important and insignificant. I had great respect for all nature—and immense pride in being even a minuscule part of earth, sky, and humankind.

It took us five hours to get off the mountain and back to base camp. The first 1,000 feet of descent was made easy by sliding down the glacier on our backsides, but at one point I lost control on a steep slope. For an instant my feet were dangling over the edge of a 500-foot icy precipice. I had to crawl on my belly to safe ground. At base camp Paul asked me if I would climb again.

"No," I said quickly.

But by morning—after much of the pain and exhaustion had lifted—I had changed my mind. And by the end of the week, I was already thinking about a second climb the following summer— this time to the summit of Mount Rainier, a 14,200-foot skyscraper.

I have since climbed a half dozen peaks in the Cascades Mountain Range (including Mount Rainier). My friends, and particularly my parents, keep asking me why (at age 55) I keep climbing mountains. How can I measure my resolve or realize my promise if I am not tested? When I stretch the fabric of my comfort zone, I become more alive—and just a little more knowing.

The driving force that propels me (and many other people) to test my will is curiosity. I am curious about the mountain, about my limits, about my ability to work with others on the line when fatigue sets in and my mind becomes muddled. What is the truth? What are my limits? How can I possibly know, unless I take one more step toward the summit?

People who are committed to truth are advocates of empirical research. They test their hypotheses. They wonder about things— about nature, relationships, and interconnections, possessing a zest for life. They have little patience with superstition, coincidence, and fate.

Guardians of Democracy

Does this happen where you work? It's the noon hour. You're in the big conference room having lunch with a dozen other employees from various departments. Everyone is engaged in animated conversation—hands are flying and the laughter is natural and free flowing. Looking in from the outside, you can't help but smile: It appears that everyone is speaking at once and having a grand time in the process.

Then the president of the company arrives, and suddenly everything changes. All heads turn to the chief executive. Everyone around the oval table leans in toward the president. They listen in rapt devotion, deferring to whatever he has to say, however inane or self-serving.

What happened? How did these bright and vivacious people suddenly turn into so much obsequious mush? The answer: monarchy. Although we live in a democracy, organizations abound with people who prove that behind every great organization is a great ego. They believe that the organization is best served when all employees reverently adhere to their direction. When this happens—and it happens all too frequently—it invariably results in generating groupthink (false consensus). Individuals waste enormous energy—not to mention creativity and real problem-solving—in the continual struggle to gain approval from the monarch. There is no commitment to truth, only to royal blessings.

There are monarchial husbands and wives, fathers and mothers, brothers and sisters, ministers and teachers, coaches and managers.

Once a car salesman gave me the monarch treatment. When I walked into the showroom, this tall, well-dressed man was reading the sports section of the local newspaper.

"I was wondering if you could tell me something about your line of cars?" I asked.

"What specifically?" the salesman snapped, obviously irritated by the interruption.

I simply said, "Perhaps another time," and walked out the door and drove to the Mercedes-Benz dealership next door, where I was treated like royalty.

A monarchial ego or regal self-absorption is its own worst enemy, ultimately resulting in the dissipation of human connectedness and the tragic dismissal of human talent.

Monarchists can reverse their autocratic tendencies by encouraging individual autonomy in five ways.

1. Encourage creative thinking. Creative thinking is a self-perpetuating, natural high; few pleasures match the satisfaction of capturing a new idea. Monarchists cannot tolerate creative thinking; it interferes with their dictums. Democratic leaders encourage creative thinking because they trust the wisdom of the people. In the workplace, creativity generates more efficient and effective ways of conducting business. At home, creativity helps in resolving conflicts, disciplining children, and selecting a family activity that everyone can enjoy.

You can encourage creativity in many ways—by brainstorming, for example, or by reframing the problem in a new context: How would John Wayne solve this problem? What approach would King Solomon take? Creative approaches to problem solving are fun.

2. Encourage others to determine their own goals for success. People succeed not because they are told how to behave but because they tap the power within by setting their own goals. An inside-out approach to goal setting stimulates commitment and activates the subconscious mind. Recognizing a deep, personal need is the first step to developing commitment; we readily rally our forces to extinguish the pain of an unmet need. Moreover, something magical occurs when we articulate an internal goal: once spoken, the words seep into the subconscious mind, which works to satisfy the unmet need.

3. Invite others to appraise their own performance. Insisting that others—employees, children, spouses, and friends—evaluate their performance promotes independence and self-control. It also attests to your commitment to responsible self-direction.

In the workplace, performance evaluation should be an adult-to-adult encounter in which ideas and concerns are expressed and discussed mutually; the manager serves more as a sounding board than a correction officer.

On the home front—among spouse, children, or friends—evaluations should be eliminated. Encourage self-regulation by forming questions, instead of making statements: Try substituting "What you should have done is . . ." for "What did you think of your performance?" or "What would you do differently next time?"

4. Allow others to take the lead. Asking others to chair meetings or facilitate family discussions decreases the likelihood of groupthink. It offers others a chance to practice communication, leadership, and problem-solving skills—thereby reinforcing the development of responsibility. It also underscores your commitment to individual autonomy and respects the contributions of others.

5. Counteract deferential behavior. Sometimes the presence of a powerful person can stifle creative problem solving. When that happens, leaders need to excuse themselves from the proceedings. This is a dramatic way of demonstrating their commitment to independent thinking.

Encouraging employees or family members to take charge of the problem-solving process is not an abdication of managerial or parental responsibility. On the contrary, it is one of the most responsible tacks we can take to nurture problem-solving skills in others and to increase the number of alternatives generated.

DEDICATION TO IMPORTANCE: RELATIONSHIPS

Those with a hearty discipline of commitment are dedicated to attending to that which is most important: relationships. Can you think of anything more important? Does not all personal and professional success hinge on relationships? A student must relate favorably with classmates and teachers, a husband with wife (and visa versa), a businessperson with internal and external customers. Even in solitude, our success is dependent upon our relationship with our inner selves, and with a higher power. Our lives are inexorably intertwined in relationships. We are dependent upon relationships for a sense of well being. The happiest people seek reconciliation, turn the other cheek, and seek forgiveness. They know that their happiness depends on the health of their relationships. When I decided to marry Nita 32 years ago, my mother advised me, "Don't let the sun go down on your wrath." She knows about the importance of maintaining relationships.

Once I flew into a small southwestern airport on business and when I disembarked, I noticed that a popular movie actor was also one of the passengers. As we waited for our bags, he and I made repeated eye contact. We seemed—in this furtive way—to be building a relationship. So, as a token of friendly acknowledgement, I nodded slightly. But upon seeing that gesture, he expelled a burst of air through his nostrils and showed me the heels of his pointy-toed, alligator, cowboy boots.

Would a smile have been too much to ask for? Afterall, for 60 seconds, we had a relationship—we did relate, just not very well.

So, what does it mean to relate in a positive and nurturing way? To answer that question, we will explore relationships with family, friends, intimates, and co-workers.

Relating to Families

The quality of our relationships within families is critical to the development of heart, mind, and soul. Where you live is unimportant. How much you earn is inconsequential. What cannot be substituted are family tenderness, love, and forgiveness.

Dad has always played harmonica. I remember him sitting in the Lazyboy, his feet propped up, playing the melody line to the Harmonicats purring on the Magnavox console.

At that time, Dad had only one harmonica—a 64-note Chromonica. When it was not being played, it lay at rest in its own high-polished, teak-wood box. Even when I was 11 years old, I knew that there was something very special about that instrument. When Dad played—his right hand fluttering over the sound hole—his breath produced a tone that was warm and vibrant.

How I wanted to hold that instrument in my hands and play one perfect note after the other. But my dad's instructions to my brother and me were clear and simple: "Do not touch this harmonica," he said, his tone resonating with indisputable finality.

So, I obeyed. Although one summer day, when my dad was at work and I was alone in the house, I lifted the instrument out of its berth and cradled it in my hands. Slowly I brought it to my mouth and pretended to play.

Not four measures into my silent concert, I stopped. "What am I doing?" I asked out loud. I quickly returned the silver treasure to its case.

Some 38 years later, I was visiting my parents. My dad and I were talking about music. When I was growing up, Dad and I never made music together. For one thing, I was a trumpet player, and harmonica and trumpet make a somewhat discordant duet. I think my dad appreciated my playing most when it drifted in over the rafters of the detached garage. But in the last few years, I have learned to accompany Dad on the piano.

That afternoon, Dad said, "Wait a minute, Son," and he escaped into his bedroom at the end of the hall. In a moment he reappeared, the prize in his hands. Although I had not seen it in over a quarter of a century, I recognized the glossy teak box immediately. "Here, Son," he said, "I want you to have this."

My childhood came rushing back and enveloped me like a cloak. "But, Dad," I said, "this is your original harmonica."

"I know," he said.

I had no more words. I sat there at the kitchen table and slowly glided my fingertips across the top of the shinny box. I opened the lid, lifted out the Hohner 64-note Chromonica, and for the first time in my life raised the mouth harp to my lips and blew a single note. My first sensation was, 38 years later, the return of my father's familiar fragrance, and I was lifted up by the scent. With my mouth still on the instrument, I turned and looked at Dad. He was smiling.

I wish that my dad and I had not taken so long to arrive at a place of community. For this I know: love is a better place.

Relating within a family means letting down your guard. It means being your real self and allowing others to be themselves. That is one thing that I have come to appreciate about my father: He has relaxed over the years. He doesn't seem to be the least intimidated or put off by what, for him, may seem a little strange (my tendency to be intense and cerebral or my proclivity for outdoor adventures, for example). He just sits back and watches. In fact, in some ways the roles have reversed. When we're jamming, I sometimes tease him about not reading music: "Come on," I tease, "get it right this time or I'll have to get a union musician." He laughs. He's sufficiently sure of himself to take the ribbing in stride. He has let his guard down, which is the mandatory precursor to an embrace.

Relating to Friends

Friendship requires the discipline of commitment, for friendship is not born, it is made. It requires time, energy, and stick-to-itiveness. When we are most ready to bolt from the relationship, that is the time to demonstrate our commitment to friends.

Friendship moves through distinct stages of development. At first everything is peaches and cream; I imagine that my new friend is everything I had hoped for. And then reality seeps in, and I begin to notice that my companion has flaws. That's when I take it upon myself to fix him. Naturally, my new friend dislikes the meddling and either fights back—noting my flaws—or turns and runs.

Friendship doesn't happen until the two release the impulse to fix each other. It is okay to talk about what you need from your friend—not unlike a married couple; it is not okay to add absolute compliance to your criteria for friendship.

Rick has charm—a certain boyishness, a propensity for adventure, a flare for the dramatic, and an everlasting reverence for romance—all of which endears him to everyone he meets. I have seen him take the sting out of an irascible store clerk in less that 60 seconds. He does it with a kitchen-white, porcelain smile and a kind of southern hospitality and respect, which is strange since Rick was raised on the south side of Chicago—one of the toughest neighborhoods in the nation.

Like everyone else, I, too, was immediately enchanted by Rick. Within the first 20 minutes of our meeting, he had regaled me with a description of his engagement, wedding, and honeymoon in Bermuda. Rick recounted the story in the same way that a novel unfolds. The background information was laid out in the voice of an impassioned narrator. But the dramatic scenes were fully acted out. Rick would jump out of his seat, hike up his pants, and launch into a full stage production, changing his voice and body stance to capture the essence of the characters. It was like watching a command performance of *Our Town* in the privacy of my own office.

My wife and I began to see a great deal of Rick and his wife Susan. We became very good friends. On weekends we would share a dinner or a movie or both. We exchanged gifts on Christmas. We even vacationed together, camping out at Mount Rainier National Park and scuba diving in Puerto Vallarta, Mexico. It was the Vallarta trip that was almost our undoing.

Rick's style was beginning to wear a little thin for me. What I enjoyed most about Rick initially—his non-stop theatrical patter—was now becoming tiresome. I suddenly realized that I, too, wanted to be an actor, and not just a passive member of the audience. But, more importantly, I wanted to be engaged. I wanted to be asked, "Allen, what do you think?" or "Allen, how are you feeling?" And then I wanted him to listen wholeheartedly.

I wanted equal airtime. I began to sense a tone of competition in our relationship. Rick and I seemed to be pecking at each other, playing a muted game of one-upsmanship. For example, after our first boat dive off Puerto Vallarta, Rick said to me while packing away his gear, "Allen, you've got to be more careful down there; you keep banging into me. Would you look out for me before you change directions? One time you almost tore the mask off my face."

This was not the first time I had heard this complaint from Rick, and frankly, I was tired of it. "Well, maybe you need to stop tailgating me," I shot back.

"You're right, it's my fault," Rick said after a beat. Although his words were charitable, I sensed that his attitude was sarcastic.

Neither of us was willing to talk about it openly. We brooded like school children, determined not to problem solve, and certainly not apologize.

The relationship was not where it should be. In fact, I was convinced that it was sick. I was sure that if the relationship were left unmanaged, it would die within the year.

What to do? I knew I wanted a mature relationship, one that would be free of competition and rich in understanding. But I was not sure that Rick could take it; maybe leveling with him would leave him bleeding. It would be so much easier to simply withdraw and let the relationship slowly die. Besides, I questioned whether Rick could comprehend the depth of my desires. After all,

I seldom saw beyond Rick's theatrical mask; perhaps he was incapable of being real. I knew I had to speak to him.

"Rick, I've got to talk to you," I said.

"It's about Puerto Vallarta, isn't it?" Rick said. "I'm sorry about that. I hope we're still friends."

Maybe he did understand, I thought. "I've got to talk to you," I repeated, "face-to-face."

We scheduled Sunday morning at my house. When Rick arrived, I directed him to the den.

"Rick, I'm not satisfied with our relationship," I said, "And I want to try to express exactly how I feel."

"Okay," Rick said.

"I think that immature relationships are riddled with fight-or-flight behavior. People either beat up on each other—physically or emotionally—demonstrating how one is better than the other, or they run and hide, fearful of saying what is in their hearts. I think we have been doing a lot of both. When we get together, our competitiveness jumps out. We play one-upsmanship, and I don't want to play anymore."

"I don't either," Rick said.

"We run and hide when we need to demonstrate some courage and talk through our differences."

"Yes. I understand."

With that introduction, I related a number of examples, and we talked through each one them.

"I want us to talk openly with each other about our deepest concerns and our greatest joys. I want us to be noncritical of each other, to get out of the business of judging. I want us to seek only to understand, not to admonish or preach to each other. I want us to get to the core of who we are, without stomping on each others beliefs. I want our relationship to be a sanctuary of security and love for us both."

"I want the same thing," he said. "Allen, you are not just my best friend, you are family. I do not give up on family. I love you, Allen. I will do whatever it takes to make this relationship work."

How do you like that? I thought. The student has become the teacher. Suddenly, I felt ashamed, for I was all too eager to give up on my brother, to walk away in silent resentment. What was the matter with me?

Rick was right; you do not give up on family, for at the core— underneath all the artifice, all the differences in talent, preferences, ideology, underneath all that—we are as much family as if we had come from the same womb.

Relating to Intimates

Healthy adults are committed to intimacy: an unrestrained, transparent, and vulnerable way of being. Intimacy is giving of one's self, while simultaneously receiving another—totally, without reservations. Although sex and intimacy are not exclusive of each other, they also are not synonymous, for intimacy occurs whenever two or more human beings decide to be absolutely authentic.

I have known Carole for 10 years. In that time we have become good friends. We have shared with each other some of our most deeply held thoughts and feelings—our ambitions, our concerns, even our quests for spiritual development. I feel calm and confident in her presence, all of which made her recent confession all the more perplexing.

I saw Carole at a small discussion group that meets once a month. Not having seen her for a number of weeks, I walked over to give her a hug. Just as I was about to wrap my arms around her, she shifted her body to the side and extended one arm around my shoulder—a side hug.

"What's with this side-hug business?" I protested.

"Well, I'm a kind of a side-hug person," Carole said. "I don't know what it is about me. I can hug a lover—no problem. It's just hard for me to hug a friend."

I had the feeling that Carole was confusing intimacy with sexuality. "They are not the same," I told her. "Sexuality is physical, intimacy is spiritual. Intimacy among friends—without sexuality—is splendid; it feeds our souls. Sex with a lover—without intimacy—is a travesty; it always diminishes the relationship."

I wondered if Carole was afraid to be intimate outside of a sexual experience. And if her sexual relationships were void of intimacy. Intimacy is exhibited only in those who are at peace with themselves. The willingness to be vulnerable—a requirement of intimacy—cannot be tolerated by those with fragile self-esteem; if I feel that I am unworthy, I can not, will not, give myself to you. That is one reason why it is so important to develop all five of the disciplines of effectiveness; they give us strength to love ourselves, so that we can then love others.

Relating to Co-workers

In relating at work, we must attend to two components: the relationship and the task. To attend to one and not the other is to court failure. To focus solely on relationships turns the workplace into a country club; to focus solely on task turns the workplace into a slave galleon.

The Relationships at Work. The workplace should be a school for adults. It should be a place where learning opportunities are abundant. When learning becomes stagnate, the company leaders should take steps to create learning excursions. In the ideal workplace, managers see themselves as teachers, mentors, coaches, guides; their mission is to develop competent and ethical employees. They should never lose sleep when they are off the job on travel or vacation, because they know that their associates are fully qualified to takes the reins.

In turn, the employees are insatiable learners. They seek new, uncharted waters. Although they are willing to stick to a repetitive task on the short haul, they become bored with routine. They want more for themselves and more for the company. In the best organizations, employees that feign or avoid learning are discharged.

The Tasks at Work. Not all work is productive. Sometimes our days are filled with inane email messages and rambling meetings. We know what tasks are important—projects that enhance the company mission—and, yet, repeatedly, we are besieged by work that is mindless and unproductive.

Productive workers are disciplined workers. They are hard-nosed about tending to tasks that are mission-driven. They are impatient with political policies that are more a product of managerial puffery than good business sense. They insist on doing the right thing: serving the values and mission of the organization and enhancing internal and external relationships.

I created what I call the *mission-driven decision tree* to help managers accomplish two objectives: ensure employee learning and focus on doing what is important. The decision tree asks five questions:

1. *Is it important?* If the company didn't already do this, would we do it now? Many times organizations operate out of tradition or habit. Sometimes those traditions are meaningful; sometimes they are not. Disciplined managers and employees alike examine the activity—even the sacred cows—and ask if it is still worth doing.

2. *What would happen if I did nothing?* Sometimes ignoring a task, however meaningless, can jeopardize a career. However, discretely challenging the purposefulness of an assignment with the owner of the task is sound business. Upon reflection, the task-keeper may agree that the assignment needs to be dropped.

On the other hand, the task-keeper may think the activity is still worthwhile. In that case, ask how the task advances the mission of the department, division, or organization. The question is direct and may cause the task advocate to rethink his or her position, or the advocate's response may cause you to rethink your position.

3. *Is someone else better suited to do the job.* Taking on a task just because it is on the top of the in-basket or the first thing offered is a good example of mindlessness. Someone else may be better suited—someone who is faster and more skilled at completing the task. The brightest employees utilize the diverse spectrum of expertise that is present within the organization.

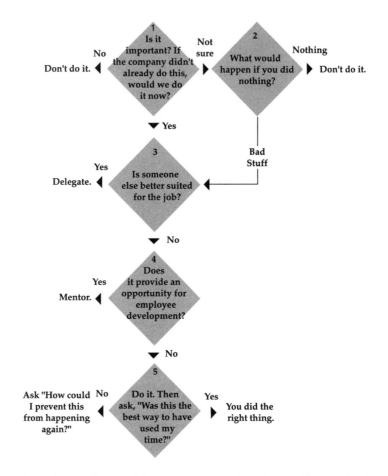

4. Does the task provide an opportunity for employee development? Generally, we are conditioned to take on whatever tasks cross our path—to prove ourselves. But once our competence and character are in tact, we have a responsibility to pass on the torch of learning opportunities. This gives an associate a chance to excel in a new arena, and it allows the senior employee to engage in activities that are better suited for his or her level of expertise.

5. Was this the best way to have used my time? Sometimes we simply must do the task. But was it the best use of our time? If the answer is no, we need to explore what we can do today to stop or divert the assignment of questionable activities tomorrow. That may mean writing a new procedure or streamlining a process or coaching an associate.

The purpose of the mission-driven decision tree is not to sidestep work, but to tackle meaningful work that best serves the company by capitalizing on individual strengths. That commitment requires a disciplined mind.

Procrastination, the nemesis of personal discipline, makes weasels out of us all; it sneaks up on us in the dark and steals away with our best intentions. Procrastination is the willful avoidance of beneficial activities. We play an active role in the game of avoidance. Procrastination is not thrust upon us; we are not victims of procrastination. Rather, we are its creators.

Procrastination is not only willful, but malevolent; it deters us from that which is most beneficial: physical, mental, relational, and spiritual fitness. Procrastination is not living; it is putting in time. How we handle procrastination has a powerful influence on our lifestyle. If we let procrastination take hold, we become a passionless observer.

The Lifestyle Matrix

The Lifestyle Matrix illustrates the components of four life choices, the least powerful of which is procrastination. To help you understand the Lifestyle Matrix, I need to define two terms:

Adventure. Adventure is the passion for experience and learning. Those who score high in adventure are perpetual students. Their lives are like a spiraling staircase—each new learning experience builds upon the previous rung. They do not stand still. In contrast, those who score low in adventure live as though life were a closed loop: an endless repetition of the same thoughts, feelings, and behaviors. They live their lives robotically, mindlessly—constrained by their own fear of the unknown or the unfamiliar.

Tenacity. Tenacity is the stick-to-it capacity—the will to stay with an activity or a relationship. People of tenacity endure the awkward early stages of development. They delay their gratification: they know that a task is rarely perfectly executed on the first attempt. Likewise, they realize that a relationship requires a great deal of nurturing to mature. So they endure early bumblings for the sake of greater learning to come.

Those who score high in tenacity are achievers and finishers. They get the job done: they earn their degrees, they work through conflicts, they turn weakness into strength. Those who score low in tenacity give up at the first sight of rough water. They are into instant gratification. If the task requires sustained effort, they look for an easy way out. They bounce around from job to job, from person to person, searching for the course of least resistance.

Tenacity and morality must go hand in hand. When morality is wanting, tenacity is another word for sociopathy. To be of value, tenacity must be directed toward behavior that is aligned to universal principles of goodness.

No one falls entirely into one quadrant. We choose exploration (or thrill seeking, procrastination, or fanaticism) in some of life's sectors, some of the time. But suppose that we discover the definitive thrill seeker, procrastinator, fanatic, and explorer. If given a platform to expound their position, what might they say?

Adventure

	Low	High
High	Fanaticism	Exploring
Low	Procrastination	Thrill seeking

The Lifestyle Matrix

The fanatic (low adventure, high tenacity): I have discovered the only way. There is no other way, and you will not be complete until you have discovered the only way too. I like the only way: it's formal, regimental, institutional. It has a floor and a ceiling and sturdy walls. It makes me feel safe. Oh, yes, I'm committed to the only way 100 percent. I will always be committed, because, after all, there is nothing else to learn, now is there? My motto is "If it ain't broke, don't fix it."

The thrill seeker (high adventure, low tenacity): Hey, man, life's a gas. Things are happening. I've got stuff to do and people to see. I'm into experiences. Don't ask me what I've learned. Life is not about learning or education; it's about doing. I want to feel good, right now, this minute. I'm not into pain. I want to get high, and I do it whatever way I can: booze, pills, sex—whatever it takes. I've been married five times, and I'm loving it. My motto is "You only live once."

The procrastinator (low adventure, low tenacity): I really don't like to talk to people about myself. You see, if I talk—if I tell you who I am—I'm afraid that you won't like me, and if you don't like me, I'd rather not know it. I guess that's why it is so difficult for me to start something. What would happen if I jumped into an important venture, and I failed? That would be awful; I don't think I could stand that. So I'd rather not try. That way I can hold on to the illusion: I could do it if I wanted to; I just don't want to. My motto is "Why risk it?"

The explorer (high adventure, high tenacity): I love new experiences. I get a kick out of life. I'm passionate about learning—it's exciting for me. The world is a playground of experiences and wonder, and I want to be a active participant. That doesn't mean, however, that I dart from one experience to the other. I like to stick it out for awhile, to find out what the experience is really like. I like to become a master at a task before I move on; that way I have a truer understanding of its essence. In fact, with some things (science, the arts, faith, family and close friends) I hold on for a lifetime. Why? Because there is so much more to learn, and I know I have just scratched the surface. Some people call me courageous, some people call me disciplined. I just don't want to sit on the sidelines and watch the parade march by. My motto is "Live life completely, without reservation: be a student of life and make a difference."

HOW TO BECOME AN EXPLORER

I favor explorers. They enter the world with eyes wide open—constantly experiencing the joy of discovery. So what would it take for those who are stuck in another quadrant to make the transition to exploration? Here are a few ideas.

From Procrastinator to Explorer

The life of the procrastinator is void of adventure and tenacity. Procrastinators are like rag dolls. They never fulfill their dreams—in fact, they never even try. They live lives of fear. They are not unlike those who suffer from avoidant personality disorder, an abnormality characterized by intense feelings of inadequacy and social inhibition. Fearing criticism or rejection of any kind, these people avoid meaningful interpersonal contact. They recoil from new activities that appear risky or potentially embarrassing.

To become explorers, the procrastinators must take a risk. This may require the help of a good friend or a competent counselor. Procrastinators must sample a few wonders of the world—despite their nagging self-doubts. They must learn to boldly talk back to the small, inner voice of negative commentary: "Shut up, I'm not listening to you."

Sample Activity List
- Seek out a friend or counselor who will encourage you on your journey to exploration.
- Make a small promise to yourself—a task or a way of being—at the end of the day. Write it down and then make it happen.
- Announce to a friend or co-worker your intention to accomplish a difficult task. Then make a luncheon date with your friend that coincides with the project's completion date. Why? To celebrate your success, of course.
- Have an adventure: take a trip abroad; go for a week-long hike or bicycle ride through a national park; sleep outside in the backyard with a friend or lover and watch the stars come out.

- Take a course of interest at a local college or university—that requires both adventure and tenacity.

From Thrill Seeker to Explorer

The thrill seeker has a high need for sensation: they love chocolates, first kisses, and fast cars. So what's wrong with that? Nothing. All three examples are delicious, but sensation is just half the story. The pursuit of sensation can become an addiction, as deadly as any drug. Like an addict, the thrill seeker is continually in the hunt for the next rush. In time no sensation can satisfy thrill seekers—they become numb, their senses over saturated and frazzled. In the end, they feel a sense of dread and emptiness, a feeling of unfathomable boredom.

In the extreme, thrill seekers are like those who suffer from manic-depression, with mood swings ranging from feelings of grandiosity to hopelessness. One symptom is an excessive indulgence into activities that offer instant gratification, but painful consequences: freewheeling shopping sprees, sexual indiscretions, or foolish business ventures. Thrill seekers frantically run from event to event, party to party, lover to lover, in a downward spiraling attempt to extinguish their ennui.

For thrill seekers to move to exploration, they must develop the quality of stick-to-itiveness. They must learn to select a noble venture and commit to its development. The thrill seekers must reverse the flow of energy: to stop feeding their own senses and begin feeding the senses of others. They must begin exploring the depth of relationships.

Sample Activity List
- Develop a deep friendship. Put in the time.
- Start a fellowship group and stick to it.
- Become involved in a community building project and see the construction through to its completion.
- Read a book on personal growth—from cover to cover.
- Join a club of interest and work up the ranks until you serve as president.

- Plan a cross-country trip—all the details—and see it through.
- Learn a new skill—something that requires time to master: water colors, rock climbing, scuba diving, Japanese gardening, car restoration. Become good enough to become a teacher—and then teach.

From Fanatic to Explorer

A fanatic is anyone who mindlessly latches on to a single view of the world. That view may assume any shape—both noble and ignoble. In the beginning, fanaticism does not grow out of evil purposes—just the opposite. The individual merely wishes to trade personal chaos—unhappiness, boredom, loneliness, self-doubt—for some kernel of meaning.

Flaming fanaticism is akin to an obsessive-compulsive mental disorder: the individual is plagued with recurrent, unwanted ideas (obsessions), accompanied by an urge to take some repetitive action (compulsion) to relieve the anxiety caused by the obsession. For example, some obsessive-compulsives have the unremitting thought that germs are everywhere and counter by repetitively washing their hands. Similarly, fanatics might hold fast to the reassuring idea that a political or religious leader is the true messiah and outrightly ignore or discredit all competing ideology.

The mind continually processes ideas for escaping personal chaos. Sometimes the ideas are unethical or immoral (those who are socially responsible quickly discard those notions). More often the ideas have some essence of truth—but not the whole truth; when a seeker pursues the idea as if it were the whole truth, you have the potential for fanaticism. On the surface the thought may appear entirely innocuous:

- Building a muscular body
- Watching television
- Surfing the net
- Going fishing
- Reading romance novels

- Seeking solace in a community

These pursuits are innocent enough. But they can become pernicious if they are followed at the exclusion of all other inquiries. Even a good thing—attention to diet, for example—can become twisted into anorexia or bulimia if allowed to become an obsession. Likewise, the apparent goodness of an honored doctrine can—when mindlessly practiced—turn into something horrific.

To become an explorer, fanatics must keep their options open. They must continue to learn, to put their belief systems to the test. That is not easy for the fanatic, since fanaticism grows out of the need to escape chaos. It is a scary thing to challenge the ideas that have provided structure and given comfort. So, what is one to do? Here are some ideas.

Sample activity list
- Develop a friendship with someone who challenges your view of the world.
- Take a course in debate: learn to understand and defend the virtues of both sides of an issue.
- Look at yourself holistically: body, mind, heart, and soul. Intentionally nurture that which is neglected.
- Challenge your own thinking by reading books or attending meetings that counter your position.
- Listen wholeheartedly. Try to understand when you are tempted to dismiss or devalue the other person.
- Take a vacation from your obsession. For two weeks turn off your mind to the old ways of doing things. Start fresh: find meaning in a new activity or assemblage of people.

THE PSYCHOLOGY OF EXPLORATION

From a psychological perspective, the explorer is self-actualized, which, according to Carl Rogers, is "the inherent tendency of the organism to develop all its capacities in ways which serve to maintain or enhance the organism." Explorers are, indeed, engaged in sustained and steady learning and, as a consequence of that behavior, enhance their sense of well-being. Rogers suggests that this tendency toward self-actualization is "inherent" in the individual. It is our natural right. Unfortunately, the thrill seekers, procrastinators, and fanatics have been derailed to believe—through poor parenting, environmental conditioning, or self-deception—that self-actualization is not their birthright. That is a cruel and paralyzing lie.

Procrastination is alluring—as are thrill seeking and fanaticism. These behavioral styles satisfy basic needs for safety (procrastination), sensation (thrill seeking), and meaning (fanaticism). But they are insidious choices, for they deter us from living lives of extraordinary vitality and richness—qualities that can only be experienced within a lifestyle of exploration.

THE LANGUAGE OF COMMITMENT

The discipline of commitment encompasses two ideals: a dedication to truth and importance, especially the importance of relationships. The language of commitment echoes that pledge.

Dedication to truth
- I am a learning machine.
- I consider all the options, even the unconventional ones.
- What I feel, think, say, and do are all one.
- I keep my word.
- I'm listening.

Dedication to importance (relationships)
- I give you my pledge to . . .
- I do what is important.
- I'd love to get together with you. How about next Thursday for lunch?
- I'm a good listener.
- I only offer advice when solicited.
- I am a mission-driven employee.

THE ACTIVITIES OF COMMITMENT

Commitment is the discipline of action. When we act, we prove that we are for real. The following actions will say more about a person's character than mere words.

Dedication to truth
- I seek the perspectives of others.
- In politically tense situations, I appoint devil advocates to challenge the group's thinking.
- I pick a flavor of ice cream never tried before.
- I challenge my own paradigms.
- I sleep on the opposite side of the bed—just for a change.
- I pick new places to vacation.
- I take college classes on subjects that are new to me.
- I sing in public.
- I am learning to play a new musical instrument.
- I always have a book in progress.
- I look for new ways of expressing intimacy to loved ones.
- I explore unfamiliar cultures.

Dedication to importance (relationships)
- I schedule time for people I care about.
- I take my wife on a date each week.
- I call my mom and dad.
- I make a conscious effort to make friends.
- I seek intimacy.
- I'm truly present when others are speaking to me.
- I say "no" to work projects that don't advance the company's mission.

PUTTING COMMITMENT TO WORK

Make a list of your greatest strengths and most glaring weaknesses. Then, create a list of the people who make you feel somehow uneasy. Now, of those people, select the one with whom you would most like to build a stronger, more relaxed relationship—clearly, someone that you care about. Call that person and ask if you could get together for a drive or a walk in the country.

When you are alone, tell the person that you genuinely want a better relationship. Explain that you think that the problem may be that you probably have a superficial understanding of the other. Share your list of strengths and weaknesses with your friend—making it clear that you want to honestly share your self-view. Then, invite the other to participate by disclosing his or her view of you. What does the other see that you don't see? The other's perspective is his or her truth. Can you live with that added information?

When you disclose freely and accept the perceptions of others without defensiveness, the other will open up—to share his or her strengths and weaknesses. All of this dialogue will be replete with understanding and commitment to truth.

Chapter 9

THE DISCIPLINE OF SERVICE

THE PATH OF MERCY AND GRACE

Lord, make me an instrument of Thy peace.
Where there is hatred, let me sow love;
Where there is injury, pardon;
Where there is doubt, faith;
Where there is despair, hope;
Where there is sadness, joy.

O, Divine Master,
Grant that I may not so much seek
To be consoled as to console;
To be understood as to understand;
To be loved as to love;
For it is in the giving that we receive;
It is in pardoning that we are pardoned;
And it is in dying that we are born to eternal life.

—St. Francis of Assisi

Jim Devine has been a friend for over 40 years; we used to play little league baseball at the city park when we were kids. So, when Jim asked if I would attend the memorial service for his father, James Sr., I quickly accepted.

Jim, a licensed minister, conducted the service. It was a very relaxed ceremony. Jim simply invited the audience to celebrate with the family by sharing positive remembrances of James Sr. Jim's father was one of the most scholarly and, yet, gentlest men I have ever met. It took no effort to praise his life. The tributes came freely, with much affection and good humor. And then Jim concluded the service by telling this story.

Many days during the summer of my 11th year were spent at a swampy pond off the Columbia River. Several of my friends and I were determined to build a sturdy raft to take us down the powerful Columbia River. But one day, I did not go to the pond. I decided to spend the day at the park playing baseball. All the guys from the neighborhood were there. We chose up sides and played a three-game series. By the time we had finished, the sun was dropping behind the Horse Heaven Hills. I felt good; I had hammered a line drive to right field to bring in the winning run.

At that moment I was oblivious to time and to the anxiety that was mounting at my home two miles away. It was now dusk, and I was nowhere to be found.

My father walked to the front porch and called my name, but there was no answer. My father knew that I was building a raft at the pond, and he was seized by the unshakable conviction that I was in danger. He rushed out of the house and raced off for the pond.

He saw no one there, only the makeshift raft. He scrambled down the embankment and waded chest high into the murky water. Again he called my name and searched the shoreline. Finally, unable to see for darkness and tears, my father returned to the house, praying that I had returned home.

I walked into the house—the most carefree of boys—only a moment after my father had returned from the pond. My baseball bat was slung over my shoulder, my mitt dangling from the end of the bat. My father's back was to me as I opened the screen door. "Hi, Dad," I chirped. "We had a great . . ."

When my father turned around, I was shocked at the sight of him. His clothes were drenched, his stock of red hair matted down, and his face had a look of despair and joy, terror and relief. In an instant he swept me up in his arms. "I love you, Son. I love you so much," my father said, pressing me tight against his chest. He kissed me again and again and whispered in a voice full of yearning, "Son, you've come home."

Jim and I had arranged to get together the day after the memorial service. We sat in my den and talked for hours about the importance of living lives of courage and deliberateness. I was taken by Jim's maturity: his love for family, his wish to be of service to others. At one point I told him how much I was moved by the story of his father.

"That is a story of grace and mercy," Jim said.

"What do you mean?" I asked.

Jim smiled. "Grace and mercy are the opposing sides of the same coin," he said. "You see, grace is the act of loving others, even when their behavior is unlovable. Mercy is the will and ability to withhold criticism or scorn—punishment of any kind—even when the behavior of the other warrants sanction."

As I reflected on his words, he offered this further explanation. "My father demonstrated both grace and mercy on that summer day. My actions—marching off for the day without the slightest notification—was hardly deserving of appreciation. And, yet, my father took me into his arms and loved me. 'You've come home,' he said. 'You've come home.' That is grace: to be loved unconditionally—even when the other is unlovable.

"And then there is mercy," Jim went on to explain. "On that day, I was overdue for a swat on the behind or, at the very least, a severe dressing-down. But my father withheld all comeuppance. I had it coming, but, instead, he lavished me with kisses.

"You see, Allen, grace is what you give to another, unconditional love; mercy is what you withhold, punishment. No other qualities are more sacred."

And, no other qualities more difficult to practice. There is only one power on earth that has the command to activate grace and mercy: Love.

• • •

I have created a matrix of Jim's thinking—a service matrix I call it—to clarify the difference between mercy and grace.

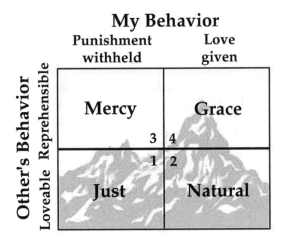

My Behavior

Living a life of mercy and grace is a steep climb. In the low lands (quadrants 1 and 2), withholding punishment (contempt, condemnation, criticism) and extending love to those who are lovable is relatively easy—it is a just and natural thing to do. But the high ground of mercy and grace (quadrants 3 and 4) is gained by withholding punishment and proffering love when the behavior of the other is reprehensible; that's a vertical climb and takes extraordinary discipline of service to achieve.

The discipline of service—as embodied in mercy and grace—rubs against our nature. Instinctively, we want to be right; we want to get even. Forgiveness and turning the other cheek do not come by *nature*, but *nurture*, through consistent and incremental steps: understanding, tolerance, and unconditional love.

Turning the other cheek does not mean we are supposed to roll over and die. It is not about being a victim, a human doormat; it is, however, about being understanding when others are under pressure, tolerant when others take a different view, loving when others resist being loved. It takes courage to turn the other cheek, to live a live of mercy and grace.

A Life of Mercy

A school playground is a microcosm of the human experience: laughter, tears, and a plethora of small conflicts. How do children deal with those conflicts? Often, they will return insults with insult; they will trade punches; they will seek retribution. Some, even turn to guns for revenge.

Like the schoolyard, the workplace offers abundant examples of retaliation: sarcasm, one-upsmanship, backbiting, silence, and withdrawal. So, how do we nurture the quality of mercy (withholding judgment and punishment) within an environment replete with hostility, oppressions, and insults? The answer is through the employment of the first four disciplines: love, responsibility, vision, and commitment.

Mercy through Love

Love is embodied in the expression of intellectual and spiritual growth for self and others. There is nothing intellectually or spiritually productive about retaliation; in fact, there is a negative correlation: as retribution mounts, intellectual and spiritual capacity diminishes. Every word of criticism I utter, every rolling of the eyes, every clucking of tongue at the expense of another human being, diminishes my spiritual centeredness.

As the 20th century French philosopher and theologian Pierre Teilhard de Chardin has said, "We are not human beings having a spiritual experience; we are spiritual beings having a human experience." Although our most primitive instinct is to get even, our human mission is to personify our spiritual heritage. The more we live a life of mercy, the more we are fulfilling our destiny.

Mercy through Responsibility

Responsibility is evoked in the freedom to make choices based on principles, regardless of the situation. Most anyone can do the right thing when there is little pressure to do otherwise. But to do the right thing when we are rebuked is the real test of our human spirit. The person with a well-developed discipline of responsibility has that inner strength.

Responsibility is not a feeling; it is not even an attitude. It is an action, a deliberate choice. In the beginning, it may have to be imitated. As novices in responsibility, we may have to pretend to do the right thing when we are, for example, the target of road rage. Despite feeling rage, the responsible person lets it go. And then lets it go again. Over time, what was once feigned tranquility and responsibility will become authentic, congruent responsibility.

Mercy through Vision

People of vision pursue missions that are noble and revolutionary. What is more noble and revolutionary than living a life of mercy? They are the true champions: the unflagging advocates of love, peace, and forgiveness—people who march, not for power or hubris, but for justice in a world that can be unbelievably cruel.

People with a revolutionary vision of nobility are not diverted by petty agendas. They remain kind and calm in the face of adversity, because their eyes are on a higher goal. These people are not Pollyanna's; they are warriors, and their swords are truth and virtue. What is more powerful than a man or woman who is on a noble quest? They appeal to us all—from the fictional Don Quixote to the very real Nelson Mandela—people who have chosen the higher road. They have the power within.

Mercy through Commitment

Those who personify the discipline of commitment are dedicated to truth and importance, especially the importance of relationships. To be dedicated to truth, to understand the rest of the story, invariably evokes mercy. The more we know about the situation, and the more we understand the players, the more we are willing to forgive.

Naturally, those who are dedicated to relationships are more willing to grant mercy. Why? Because those with a relationship-orientation seek ways to build up, not tear down, the esteem of others. Retribution does nothing to enhance self-worth, and people of commitment know that; they are more likely to forgive, and through their forgiveness help the "offender" see, by example, a better way.

Mercy toward the individual should not suggest advocacy of irresponsible behavior. One example of this distinction is the story of the adulterous woman, as told in the Gospel of John. The scribes and Pharisees told Jesus that the woman had been caught in adultery and by law should be stoned to death. Jesus countered that whoever was without sin should cast the first stone. That was too much for everyone's conscience, and all turned away. In a few moments Jesus was left alone with the woman.

"Where are your accusers?" Jesus asked. "Has no man condemned you?"

"No man," the woman responded.

"Neither do I," Jesus said. "Go and sin no more."

Jesus stood boldly for mercy (against the convention of the day), and he pressed for a change in the woman's behavior. He demonstrated a fierce commitment to the person, coupled with an equally intense commitment to promoting responsible behavior. Mercy without careful scrutiny of behavior is as irresponsible as advocating no mercy at all.

The Inheritance of the Unmerciful

I had been on the road for about a week, and upon returning home I was beat. All I wanted was a hot shower, a glass of orange juice, and the newspaper. When I entered the driveway, about one o'clock in the afternoon, I was puzzled to see our other car, a Lexus, parked inside the garage. Nita, a first-grade teacher, should have been in class.

I got out of the car, walked into the den, and turned on the answering machine.

"Hi, honey, it's me," the voice was Nita's. She sounded a little strange. "You're probably wondering why the car is parked in the garage," she continued. "Well, I tipped over some coffee yesterday when I was going to work. Some of it spilled into the gearshift. It was okay yesterday, but this morning it locked up. Sorry honey. . . . Welcome home."

I called Bob, our regular mechanic, who had just spoken to Nita a few minutes earlier. In a couple of hours, Bob came to our house and, with the counsel of a Lexus mechanic on the phone, managed to remove the console, revealing a coating of chocolate-flavored cappuccino, which had taken on the consistency of caramel epoxy.

"Can you believe this?" I said to Bob, trying to control the consternation in my voice.

"Yes, I can," Bob said, "You must feel frustrated. But, you know, Nita was really shook up."

His unspoken message was clear: "Allen, calm down; it was an accident, so don't take it out on her."

I hate it when my mechanic is right.

Just then Nita's ride pulled up at the garage door. I spotted her just as she was getting out of the car. As she approached me, she had the look of a little girl who had just spilled her milk.

At that instant I knew what was the right thing to do. I smiled and walked directly to her. I put my arms around her and kissed her. "Hi, Honey," I said. "I sure missed you."

"Hi, Sweetheart. I'm really sorry," Nita said, with sorrowful eyes—that puppy-dog look of complete innocence and bewilderment.

"I know," I said. "Don't worry about it. Bob's fixing it. I think he almost has it." Bob was able to engage the gearshift. Then I drove the car to his shop, where he thoroughly cleaned the parts and reassembled the console. The car was good as new.

It's not unusual for Nita to be playful and loving, but for the next three days she was especially affectionate. Although, we didn't talk about it, we both knew that my choice to take the small adversity in stride was a way of saying, "I love you. You are more important to me than any material possession."

As it turned out, this incident added to the "cement" of our relationship. But it didn't have to turn out that way. What if I had allowed the situation to dictate my mood? What if I had shot my mouth off? Mercy is a better choice. We are too often derailed by inconsequential events. Maybe we need to recognize that inconvenience is nothing more than the perfect opportunity to practice mercy.

A LIFE OF GRACE

Grace does not concern what is *withheld*, but what is *given*: unconditional love. The climb to maturity gets no steeper than when we are scaling the sheer cliffs of grace. We so want to be right, to create a world that is perfectly suited to us—namely, a world in our own image. To have our faces rubbed in alternative perspectives is hard to bear.

Living a life of grace is not a destination; it is a journey. No one lives a life of perfect grace, but those who are grace-centered strive everyday to treat others with honor and deep respect—even those who engage in deplorable behaviors—by deploying the disciplines of love, responsibility, vision, and commitment.

Grace through Love

Toward the end of the Civil War, Abraham Lincoln spoke sympathetically of the rebel soldiers. At the end of the speech, a staunch Unionist approached the president and chastised him for taking such a charitable position.

"You should not be speaking kindly of the enemy," the woman said. "You should be talking about destroying your enemy."

"But, madam," the president said, "would I not destroy my enemies by making them my friends?"

What would happen if we were to love our enemies? Certainly, it would defuse the enemy; it could not help but touch the heart of the other. But, more importantly, what would it do for us? To love an enemy is the antithesis of ego.

There is nothing magical about loving; it is not something that happens to us: It is something we do. To love an enemy (or anyone) is a deliberate action, no less deliberate than feeding ourselves. How do we live a life of grace? We act it moment by moment, day by day.

Grace through Responsibility

I define *responsibility* as the freedom to make choices based on principles, regardless of the situation. Given that definition, is not grace another form of responsibility?

When you choose revenge, how does your body feel? When you choose resentment or sarcasm, what goes on under your skin? The physiology of anger offers a prime example: The brain releases the hormone noradrenalin, which is pumped directly into the heart, causing it to blast into high gear, working five times harder than normal. At the same time, blood vessels throughout the body constrict (forcing blood into muscles to serve a fight-or-flight instinct), dramatically raising blood pressure. Your body is well equipped to tell you when you are off kilter.

How do you live a life of grace? Make choices that result in a body that is peaceful and tranquil.

Grace through Vision

The aphorism tells us that "As a man thinketh in his heart, so is he." If our character is the sum of our collective thoughts, then what we think will either diminish or augment our grace.

To live a life of grace is *to think* a life of grace. That means being vigilant sentries of our thoughts. Our senses are bombarded by stimuli: sights, sounds, and sensations of all varieties. Some of those sensations are worthy of contemplation; others warrant nothing more than the casual observation. A wayward thought does not even deserve the dignity of formal escort out the door.

Recently, I spoke to a friend who works with people who are addicted to pornography: people who, despite the danger, will log on to Internet pornography over 50 times each day. They know it is not right; they know their careers are at risk; and, yet, they continue. For many, the addiction started in their adolescence and escalated through their adult years, becoming all consuming. Although the condition is tragic, it is not surprising. We are what we think. For that reason, we must honor only the best of thoughts. If we are to be consumed, let us be consumed by grace.

I suggest that when we are assaulted by a deleterious thought that we literally say *no*. Whether the thought is directed inward to our perceived inadequacies or outward toward the deficiencies of others, the word is *no*. "*No*, I will not indulge in that internal snipping; *no*, I will not engage in stewing over the transgressions of others. Instead, I will replace the negative thought with a mental gift of kindness, a sacrament of grace."

Grace through Commitment

When I ask audiences to tell me what is most important to them, they almost always include family, often with a gleam of love in their eyes. There is nothing unexpected about that. But what if we were committed to our enemies (those who have wronged us or simply annoy us) with equal devotion? What if we thought of our enemies as a divine gift sent just in time to help us take the next step toward maturity? What if our enemies were really our guides?

I have a friend who is incessantly babbling about the world according to him. It can be wearing. But I think that my friend has come along at just the right time to teach me patience. He has taught me, unwittingly, to relax and let someone else shine for a change. To see others who typically annoy or anger us as a conduit to personal growth is a prodigious step into the light of grace.

A Story of Grace

A missed opportunity to manifest grace in difficult times need not end in failure; there is always a second chance for redemption through reconciliation and forgiveness.

Earlier, I mentioned that my wife and I taught English as a foreign language in Algeria for two years (1973 and 1974). In the spring of our first year I wrote to a friend who was running keno at Lake Tahoe. The previous year, she was a high school English teacher. Running keno was, to my mind, a waste of her talent. I told her that in a letter, and invited her to join my wife and me in Algeria, where I was sure I could get her on as an instructor.

Within days I received her reply. She was coming.

Kathy stayed with us in a two-story, stucco building that was leased to us by Methodist missionaries who were on leave in France. My wife and I had the entire top floor to ourselves; another American, Gene, had the basement. It was a simple house, but by Algerian standards it was a mansion. Although it was invariably cold, it did have hot running water, a small refrigerator, and a stove. Kathy took the extra bedroom across the hall.

For the first six months, everything went smoothly. We thoroughly enjoyed each other's company. We often talked about books we had read, poetry we were writing, and our plans for the future. Kathy was always open and honest about her experiences and feelings. That was welcomed, but it was also our undoing. By the sixth month, I decided that she was confused, misdirected, and more liberal than I could ever tolerate. Her stance on abortion, women's liberation, and homosexuality sent me into a tirade. She ignited in me a holy responsibility to "fix her."

My irritation was not limited to Kathy's political views. Suddenly, everything about her annoyed me. We were living in rugged country, and Kathy always chose to wear hiking boots. Not a bad idea, yet I came to despise those boots. The clomping on hardwood floors exasperated me. "Why can't she walk lightly?" I asked myself. "Is she incapable of learning heel-toe, heel-toe? Is that too much to ask?"

I was on a rampage. By the end of the year, I had a hard time even looking at Kathy. Our conversations became increasingly brief and often limited to my criticism of her liberal views. That rancor endured for three more months; it is how we parted at the end of the year. I was happy to be rid of her.

For the next 25 years, Kathy haunted me. Shortly after leaving Algeria, I was sick with remorse. Kathy had been a good friend. I had been attracted to her irreverent disdain for convention, for her courage in acting on her convictions. I had destroyed what could have been a life-long friendship. How could I have behaved with so little tolerance?

A year after leaving Algeria I sent a letter of apology to Kathy. She did not reply. I tried telephoning. I spoke to an answering machine. "Please call me," I pleaded. Silence. In the end I resolved to live with my own demons.

I lost contact with Kathy for the next 20 years. I learned from Gene that she had returned to teaching, first in France and then in Japan. How typical of Kathy, always the adventurer.

And still she haunted me.

Today I travel a lot, speaking to companies and associations about, ironically, the virtues of living by principles. One of my engagements was scheduled for Boston. I knew that Gene was now living in Brattleboro, Vermont, approximately 80 miles east of Boston. I decided to spend a couple of days with him and his family before my engagement.

"I'm excited about seeing you again," Gene said. "It will be good to catch up on old times. By the way, Kathy is here in Brattleboro. She is teaching at the Language Institute. She is also looking forward to seeing you."

My heart jumped. Finally I would have a chance to see Kathy face to face and make peace.

As soon as I drove into Brattleboro, Gene called Kathy on the telephone to tell her I had arrived.

"Let me speak to her," I said.

Gene handed the phone to me. "Hello, Kathy. I just want you to get psychologically prepared for a 25-year-old hug."

Kathy laughed, rather nervously. "Whew, I don't know," she said, "we might have to take it in five-year increments."

Something in her voice sounded protective, formal. I wondered if our meeting would be awkward. Kathy arrived within the hour.

"It is so good to see you," I said with meaning. Except for the gray in her hair, she had changed very little; she was still tall, all arms and legs. Her speech patterns were familiar, like the way she would punctuate my thought with a soft "hum."

There were five of us now: Gene, his wife Fiona, their precocious daughter, Sienna, Kathy, and me. We immediately launched into a dialogue that lasted two days. We talked for hours about Algeria, travel, favorite books, philosophy, and the joy of growing older and, hopefully, wiser.

On the second day Gene, Kathy, and I went snowshoeing on the wooded hillsides that surround Gene's home. It was a beautiful day. The sky was blue and the air was calm and crisp. Along the way Gene pointed out the variety of trees that graced the hills. By the time the three of us had worked our way back to the house, we were exhausted, but very content—bonded by the ineffable beauty and mystery of nature.

On my flight home I composed a short poem for Gene that expressed the reverence I placed on the experience.

Eugene Parulis,
Priest of the forest,
Tends to his aspens, birches, and ferns.
He treads through the temple
Of yin and yang
And blesses the elders,
Parishioners all
Of New England sun.

Will you lead me, father,
Into the woods today?
Will you share this sacrament:
Summer, winter, May?

That night we sat around the dinner table and talked.

"I am enjoying this so much," Kathy said around midnight, "but I do have to go. I'm teaching a class tomorrow morning. I must get some sleep."

Not knowing if I would ever see Kathy again, I needed to make peace, now.

"Kathy, wait a minute. I need to speak to you privately."

"Sure," Kathy said, a little surprised by the request.

We settled into chairs in Gene's office, facing each other. I began, "Kathy, you have haunted me for 25 years. I have never been able to forgive myself for the way I treated you when we were in Algeria. I was uncommonly cruel to you and that fact has tormented me over the years."

"Oh, Allen."

"I feel like I crushed your spirit, and for that I am so sorry."

"Allen, it's okay." She was smiling tenderly at me. "It is not all your fault. I don't think that I have ever seen anyone experience the kind of culture shock that you went through."

Kathy caught me by surprise. Culture shock? It had never occurred to me that the upheaval of living abroad might have contributed to my behavior. At first my ego dismissed the idea, but perhaps Kathy was right. I remembered counting the days until our return to the states.

"Even if that is the case," I said to Kathy, "that is no excuse for my behavior. It is not what I am about. I do not undercut the spirit of people. I never want to do that with anyone, certainly not with you." Kathy's eyes were beginning to tear up. "I have tried to make peace with you, Kathy, but I have never felt forgiven. I feel like your ghost is still with me."

"Allen, you can put that ghost to bed. I have forgiven you for . . ."

Kathy stopped in mid sentence. She was silently crying, tears streaking down her cheeks. "I'm just so glad that we had this conversation. There was someone else that I cared for very deeply. But we never got to a place of forgiveness. And now it is too late. That person is gone."

"I'm so sorry, Kathy."

Kathy straightened up in her chair and collected her composure as quickly as she had lost it. I sensed that Kathy had bottled up a great deal of pain inside of her. She smiled. "All is well with us, Allen."

"Is it?" I asked, looking deep into her eyes.

"Yes," she said without embellishment. "Now, come here. Let's have that 25-year-old hug."

A 25-year-old hug! How we punish ourselves, when forgiveness is only a few words away. What foolishness! I do not know if all of this is closed for Kathy. She said it was, but I am not sure; my hunch is that there is something more—some injury to heal, some grievance to release. I don't know. As for me, I have taken her at her word: "You are forgiven." I am at peace. And I stand resolute that I will never again allow such pettiness to invade my spirit.

THE EMBODIMENT OF MERCY AND GRACE

We need to become ambassadors of service and contribution. Service must become our reason to be. What is the alternative? To serve self? Sure, that's important, but it is not the end; it is the means: we love ourselves so that we can better love and serve others. How can our commitment to service be expressed? I would like to share four attainable ways of being that embody the discipline of service: the deliberate formation of communities, the art of listening, the resolution of conflict, and simple acts of kindness.

1. The deliberate formation of community. In recent years, one of the most satisfying experiences of service for me has emerged in the formation of a community—a fellowship of caring people. A true community is rare and seldom evolves without a hitch or two, as the following story reveals.

One summer morning I decided to make my way up Badger Mountain—a lofty hill at the back of my house. It was a perfect morning for the hike. The wind was calm, and the air was clean and crisp. About half way up, I began thinking about my friends, particularly those special people who seem to have a healthy, positive outlook on life. What would it be like to have a half dozen of those friends in the same room? I wondered. The more I thought about it, the more I knew I had to make it happen.

As soon as I got off Badger, I sat down at my desk and wrote down six names: Cathryn, Rick, Debbie, Bruce, Dave, and Cheryl.

All six of these people had one thing in common: a joy for life. They were all fun to be around—confident, optimistic, capable.

I dashed off an invitation to join me for lunch at my home in two weeks. I told them that I just wanted the pleasure of their company. I also asked them to be prepared to answer this question: What has been your greatest learning over the last year?

The day of the luncheon arrived, and they were full of smiles and positive thoughts about personal growth and the desire to give to others. It ended all too soon. I closed by sitting down at the piano and playing a chorus of a stirring tune by Joe Raposo entitled "Winners."

Here's to the winners all of us can be.

We all had such a good time that we decided to continue meeting once every month to share our thoughts and feelings regarding our quest toward intellectual and spiritual growth. I set up the next session, complete with a new question: If you were to die today, what would have gone undone?

The second session was equally satisfying. We decided to open the meetings to anyone who wished to come. The group sessions expanded to 10 or 12 participants.

After about six months, though, I began to have some concerns. Our discussions were becoming very philosophical. Something was missing.

I began to notice that although no one disagreed in the open, critical judgments were permeating the group. Cheryl, a dear friend who sees the connectedness of all things, was starting to annoy some who had a more "down-to-earth" conviction. When Cheryl spoke, one or two people started to squirm.

About this time I was reading a book by Scott Peck, *A Different Drum*, a book about community. Peck describes four stages of development: 1) pseudo-community is the honeymoon stage, where pretense flourishes and differences are ignored; 2) chaos is where members attempt to obliterate the differences and convert others to their own standards of conduct; 3) emptiness is a place of release of prejudices, biases, and, control; and 4) community is characterized by love, forgiveness, and peace. It is a place where incredible healing takes place without anyone trying to heal.

As I read Peck's words, I began to realize that we were locked in the honeymoon stage. We had a taste for sweetness and spice, yet underneath we were seething. So, at the beginning of the next session, I introduced Peck's four stages of community to the group. "Where do you think we are?" I asked.

The group was silent for a moment and then in their inimitable style began to respond. The discussion progressed for the next 20 minutes; I recognized we were launching again into philosophical platitudes—all fine in their place, but not very helpful in advancing us to community.

"We are not a community unless we are completely transparent and accepting of each other," I said. "We are not there yet. We are wearing a cloak of deception."

Then Cheryl spoke. Her question jerked me up short; I could feel the bit buried deep into my mouth. "What do you mean *we?*" she asked.

I was silent for a long time. No one said a word. Finally, I said, "You're right. This is not about us, it is about me. It is what I want. I want a sense of community—a place of sanctuary—a place where I can feel completely at home, fully secure that anything I say, any fear or joy I express, will be received tenderly, without judgment or admonition. Other than with my wife, I don't know if I have ever felt that kind of security. I want it. I want family . . ." And with that my voice started to waver. "The bottom line for me is this: Do we want to seek community together?"

As I looked around the room I realized that I was not alone in this quest, that community was something we all sought. That night was the beginning. It was, in a way, an announcement of a new way of behaving, characterized by an absence of competition and a commitment to being authentic and compassionate.

That was the beginning of my efforts to form a community. Over time we evolved into an all-men's group that has withstood the test of time (five years as of this writing). It is a supportive band of brothers that meets twice a month for the sole purpose of experiencing community.

2. *The art of listening.* The second embodiment of the discipline of service—the tool that makes community work—is listening, one of the most exquisite gifts of service.

We are not very good at listening. What stops us from lending an ear? I think the culprits are ego and deference, neither of which have anything to do with listening.

I once worked for a burley CEO who had commanded an aircraft carrier. I clearly remember the moment we met. Six of us were clustered around the executive conference room table, having lunch. The president exploded into the room.

"What's going on here?" he bellowed.

"Oh, just high-level stuff, Chief; you wouldn't be interested," someone joked.

"Oh, yeah? I'll be the judge of that." And with that he plunged into one of the swivel chairs, surveyed the room, and stopped when he got to me. "And who might you be?" he asked.

"I might be Allen Johnson," I said.

"Watch out, Chief," the company lawyer said. "You're talking to the company shrink."

The president threw back his head and released two bursts of laughter, like canons from a gunship. "You know what, Johnson? I love having guys like you around. I love to drive you couch jockeys crazy."

"Hit me with your best shot then," I said. "Because when I'm through, you may have to see your therapist *every* day."

The point-counterpoint conversation continued for 10 minutes. We launched into a discussion of chaos theory. I was working hard to pretend that I knew what I was talking about.

At the end, the president shook my hand firmly. "It was *almost* a pleasure to meet you," he said.

All night long I thought about my introduction to the president. I was not happy with myself.

I worked late the next day. It was about 6 p.m. when I headed for the exit. On my way, I saw the president coming out of his office. I seized the opportunity to speak with him.

"Hey, I'm glad I ran into you," I said.

"Don't ever be glad to run into me," he boomed, grabbing me by the shoulder and shaking me.

I changed to a more serious tone. "You know, I have written a personal mission statement for myself."

The president winced.

"One of my statements reads, 'I have nothing to prove to others, but everything to prove to myself.' I owe you an apology."

The president raised his eyebrows.

"I violated my principles by allowing myself to compete with you," I said. "I would like to establish a relationship built on collaboration. Yesterday, I felt we were butting heads."

"Hey, there's nothing wrong with butting heads. Otherwise, things would get boring around here. You didn't hurt my feelings."

"The apology is really for me," I said.

In the middle of this conversation, Doris, a colleague of mine, wandered by and stopped to listen. She put her arm around me and said, "Those of us who work with Allen know he has to work on his sense of humor."

I stood there feeling like one lone mango in a barrel of apples.

"I want you to see something," the president said. He went into his office and returned with a photo album. "Look at this." They were pictures of the aircraft carrier he had commanded. "This is me on the bridge," he said.

Sure enough, it was the chief, wearing a brown leather jacket and teardrop sunglasses. "This is me too," he said, pointing at a jet zooming off into the wild, blue yonder.

"You were a pilot then," I said, recognizing that I had fallen into a pit of patronizing blather.

All too often our conversations ramble on like that—sparring, jabbing, weaving and bobbing—just so much ego and deference.

But it is not listening. The richest listening, empathic listening, creates an atmosphere so warm and inviting that the speaker begins to relax, become more rational, and ultimately, discover his or her own personal truth.

What is the purpose of listening? On the surface the answer seems obvious. But I'm not so sure. For many, listening takes on three distorted purposes: 1) *think time*—time to compose one's own position; 2) *trap time*—time to discern minor errors in the speaker's logic, and prepare a response; and 3) *dream time*—time to dawdle in one's own thoughts and fantasies, while maintaining a pretense of listening for the speaker's benefit.

If the purpose of listening is not that, then what is it? There are at least three: to understand, to become intimate, and to heal.

• *To understand.* The primary purpose of listening is, simply, to understand the world of the other person. Understanding—without agreeing, disagreeing, or judging—is an arduous task. It requires prodigious discipline to seek to understand when the impulse is to ignore the person or disagree with what he or she is saying. It requires a commitment to honor the perspective of the speaker, regardless of how strange or abhorrent it might sound.

• *To become intimate.* Listening is the path to intimacy, an expression of warm friendship. I am often puzzled by people's reluctance to seek intimacy. So much of our communication in business is characterized by small talk, sermons, and commands. Many business people argue that there is no place for intimacy in the workplace. I strongly disagree. An office without intimacy—without a feeling of community—is a wasteland. If our need to belong is not satisfied, we are living in a virtual dessert, dying slowly of loneliness.

• *To heal.* A small miracle occurs when one wholeheartedly listens and is listened to. Both speaker and listener begin to sort out thoughts and feelings. With time, understanding emerges; and with understanding, healing follows. That healing, whether personal or interpersonal, is made evident by more self-awareness and less conflict. Ultimately, listening is the conduit for forgiveness and friendship.

The outcome of listening to understand is to influence. The reason we are poor at listening is because we want to influence others; we want to set them straight right now. We seek to influence them before we hear them. The more people feel understood, the more they willingly seek to understand the thoughts of others. Influence is a major side benefit of listening.

When I was going to college my mother would send me a "care package" two or three times a year. The package was invariably a treasure chest of my favorite goodies. Basically it had everything a college boy needed to survive the long (and sometimes lonely) nights of studying for finals or commiserating over a derailed romance. Mom's packages were always cause for a little celebration dance around the campus mailbox.

In a way empathic listening is like a care package from home—giving us just what we need at the time: understanding. The acronym for empathic listening is CARE: clarify, arrange, rephrase, and ensure.

Clarify. Empathic listeners are serious about understanding what the other is saying. But speakers are not always clear; they

Empathic listening

Clarify
Arrange
Rephrase
Ensure

CARE

ramble, get diverted, and speak in generalities. Empathic listeners are intent on understanding what is really being said, so they ask questions for clarification—to move the speaker from the vague to the concrete. Clarifying is not probing. The intent is not to lecture, but to understand.

People tend to speak in generalities. They would like to say more, but they have learned that people usually are not interested in what they have to say; so, they say as little as possible. People usually talk about: experience (what has happened to them), behavior (what they have done), and feelings (the emotions associated with the experience or behavior). These can be overt (observable) or covert (unobservable).

As you listen, determine whether the speaker is talking about an experience, a behavior, or a feeling (or combination), and offer an "expanding phrase" to move the speaker from a vague to a concrete statement.

This process might sound like:

"Sometimes I feel like I can't do the work."
"What do you mean?"
"My boss said I was stupid. I was trying to write a project progress report, and I forgot to include a critical section on safety. I knew it was important, but for some reason I omitted it. Maybe I've got too many things going on in my life these days."

Listeners don't have to offer much to encourage the speaker to continue—just an indication that they are tuned in. Notice how the speaker's concrete description opens the door for further exploration. Sometimes, the most powerful option is to remain silent for a moment. Most people are uncomfortable with silence and want to fill the void.

Arrange. Through clarification, the sense of what the speaker is saying begins to evolve. The task of the listener is now to arrange what is being said into some semblance of order. This requires full concentration; wander for a moment and the tread of understanding is broken.

When people talk about issues that are emotionally laden, their thoughts are usually random and unorganized. They struggle to sort out what is important and what is not. Your task as the listener is to help them make the connections.

Often speakers will take a long time to say what is on their minds. Because the issues have emotional impact, they are likely to repeat their position. Because listeners are less emotionally involved, they can understand what is being said, sort through the ramblings, and organize the speaker's thoughts. They can identify the essence of what is being felt, along with the experience and behavior associated with that feeling, package it, and offer verbal feedback.

Mental arranging or packaging takes focused concentration and a willingness to sort through scrambled thoughts and feelings. Listening in this way is one of the greatest gifts that we can give to another person in need. Next to the need to survive, people want to be understood, validated, and loved. This need to be loved and understood is so powerful that it sometimes overtakes the basic need to survive. Taking the time and energy to arrange the thoughts of another person is nothing less than an act of love. It is saying, "I am here; I am listening; I am your friend."

Rephrase. Arranging is mental; rephrasing is verbal. The listener verbalizes what he or she has arranged throughout the speaker's discourse, remaining true to the speaker's intent. The listener must speak without judgment, condescension, or sympathy, acting more like a faithful translator by reflecting the feeling, experience, and behavior back to the speaker.

Rephrasing is the conversion of mental packaging into words that are clear, concise, and accurate.

Be careful to describe the feeling and the experience and behavior associated with the feeling:

"So, you feel confused about your profession because, although engineering is a family tradition, it doesn't give you much joy."

"Your promotion has been a long time coming, but you feel on top of the world tonight."

Often speakers will express contrasting emotions when they are struggling to make a difficult decision. A good listener recognizes when a speaker is expressing contrasting emotion and rephrases the speaker's bilateral thinking, either by linking the two contrasting thoughts with the conjunction *but,* or by expressing the contrasting thoughts in other words:

"You want to have the courage to tell your manager what's troubling you, *but* you fear that she'll be defensive or vindictive."

"On one hand you'd like to get this out on the table with your manager. It feels like the right thing to do. On the other hand, you're not sure that you can trust your manager. You think she may strike back in some way."

Ensure. Ensuring the accuracy of rephrasing is essential. This is a gift to the listener. It says, "I value you so much that I want to be sure that I have not distorted your meaning."

Rephrasing the speaker's thoughts accurately is more than a common courtesy; it is a validation of his or her humanity. The act is saying, "I truly want to understand, and if I have missed the mark, I want to know about it."

Ensuring your understanding does not suggest that you agree with the speaker's position, only that you understand it. If you have missed the speaker's point, quickly clarify your understanding. If you allow your mind to drift, admit it and get back into the listening groove. Traditional listeners are anxious to solve problems; in fact, they are usually ready to solve the speaker's problems even before the problem has been fully stated. It is time to move from empathic listening to problem solving when the speaker feels understood, the listener fully understands, and the speaker's tone has shifted from emotion to logic.

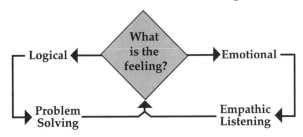

The key is to be sensitive to the emotional timbre of the speaker: If the speaker's language and tone is emotionally charged, continue to employ empathic listening. When the speaker's language and tone has become logical, try problem solving, but be ready to return to empathic listening at the first sign of emotion.

Deal with feelings first, then solutions. And solicit ideas from the speaker. Where there is involvement, there is commitment. The empathic listener wants the solution to belong to the speaker.

3. *The Resolution of Conflict.* The third embodiment of the discipline of service is the capacity to resolve conflict. Even a true community skilled in the art of listening has conflict. There is nothing subversive about conflict—it is as natural as contrasting opinions. The question is how do we resolve conflict, while maintaining an attitude of service.

Like a lifesaver—this four step model will keep any relationship afloat.

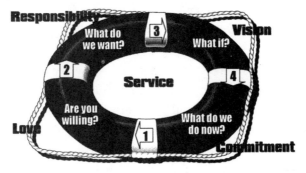

Service is at the core of my four-step conflict resolution model. Negotiators must set aside their urge to win at all costs and, instead, be resolved to create an environment of mutual respect and find a solution that satisfies the needs of all parties. That spirit ensures the durability of the solution and the dignity of the relationship.

Step 1: Love. An attitude of love is the will to engage in a journey of discovery, the key question being "Are you willing to sit down and find a solution that will satisfy both our needs?" The phrase "are you willing" suggests a respect for the agency of the other person. If he or she is unwilling to discuss the issue, you may ask, "When do you think you would be ready?" If the answer is "never," you are far from community, and you must begin the long process of developing interpersonal trust before engaging in meaningful conflict resolution.

Step 2: Responsibility. The discipline of responsibility suggests making choices based on principles. Making responsible choices begins with listening to understand. The question "What do we want?" is designed to get all needs on the table; that is a prerequisite to finding a solution that will satisfy all concerns. Allow the other to begin by listing his or her needs first because the other's agenda is held sacrosanct. Deafness dissolves as soon as one feels understood. If you want to be heard, first listen.

Step 3: Vision. The discipline of vision is the ability to visualize a noble outcome. The key question is "What if?": "What if we did it this way? Would it satisfy our needs? No? How about this way?" The question "What if?" is playful and hypothetical. There is nothing to lose in asking the question; it allows you both to explore the world of possibilities without risk. If the first approach doesn't work, so what? There are other alternatives.

Step 4: Commitment. The discipline of commitment is the willingness to do what is important to reach our mutual goals. The key questions are results-oriented: "Now that we have discovered the solution, what steps do we need to take to set it in motion? How will we monitor our progress? Should we check back in two weeks to see how we are doing?"

This conflict-resolution model is destined to succeed, because it is founded on the principles of the five disciplines. Conflict resolved through intimidation, political maneuvering, or subversive tactics provides short-lived solutions that damage the relationship.

The conflict resolution model may be applied whenever differences arise. It is a reliable tool for arriving at agreement. Opportunities for discovering creative third alternatives to resolve differences lie just beyond the horizon of our current understanding.

Most people tend to run at the first sight of conflict. Few of us have been trained in the art of discovering creative alternatives. Indeed, our culture tends to encourage the adversarial tactics of defend and attack; we see it in athletics, politics, law, education, even religion. That is why discarding positioning and embracing common-ground solutions is so effective. The question, "What if we did this?" is an invitation to become a modern-day explorer.

4. *Simple Acts of Kindness.* The fourth way to embody service is to practice simple acts of kindness. Those acts are limited only by our imagination or insensitivity to conscience. The last lines of the poem "What is Success?" by Ralph Waldo Emerson reads: "To know even one life has breathed easier because you have lived. This is to have succeeded."

My mother is a master at helping others to breathe easier. She does it through simple acts of kindness. She takes an active interest in everyone she meets. She listens with astounding concentration. She visits the sick and encourages the downhearted. She is well known for her letters of concern, kindness, and gratitude. They are always letters that lift the spirit, helping others to breathe a little easier. She is one of the most successful people I know.

My mother inspired me to begin writing letters of encouragement and gratitude to those who help me to breathe a little easier. Over the years I have written to friends who have inspired me: a librarian who served with joy, a college professor who modeled good humor and integrity. These letters have been received with overwhelming gratitude, as if to say, "For me? How incredible."

Letters have that kind of positive impact for this reason: they are intentional acts of love, requiring thought, time, and energy. Recipients are almost always flattered and emotionally stirred. If your letters are written from the heart—in the spirit of pure kindness—your readers will treasure them.

I offer two examples of such letters, hoping they may inspire you to write people who have made a difference in your life. The first was written to a neighbor, Jon Spangle, a gifted cabinetmaker who built my desk and cabinets with craftsmanship.

Dear Jon:

I love quality. I love the smell of it and the touch of it. Quality feeds the mind, heart, and, soul. It is something to be cherished. I feel it when I am at the keyboard of a fine piano. Most recently I experienced it in my own office.

Know this: for many years to come, when I sit down at my new desk to compose a letter or create a proposal or simply dream about things to come, my heart will sing, for I will do it all surrounded by the Steinway of office cabinetry.

The last time I was in Jon's shop, he showed me that the letter was still mounted proudly on his wall behind his desk.

The second letter was delivered to a mother whose son, Larry (a childhood friend), died unexpectedly of a heart attack.

Dear Larry:

I have a host of memories of you, Larry, but for some reason the remembrances that are most vivid are those that have to do with running. When you and I shared the same gym class in high school, we were instructed to run a mile race.

You and I were at the head of the pack, running stride for stride. On the fourth and last lap, all of us were compressed into a web of legs and arms. You eased forward. My lungs were burning, but I was determined to win that race whatever the cost, so I stepped up the tempo. On the final curve, I wanted the inside lane, so I edged in front of you. I cut it too close, forcing you to lose your cadence. I heard you stumble behind me, exhale, and then strain to regain your pace.

I beat you in that race by a nose, but I knew, even then, that I had won unfairly. After we had caught our breath, you walked up to me and said, "Good race, Al," and then, almost as an afterthought, "You know, you cut me off on the curve." I knew, and I said nothing. That quiet strength is what I remember most about you, Larry.

Today, I see you running on the ivy-lined roads of heaven, running your own pace—quietly, calmly, at perfect peace—and just maybe waiting for your old friend Al to join you, shoulder to shoulder, stride for stride, into the face of God.

Letters like these make a difference. They are perhaps the most extravagant gift you can give: the simple recognition of another human soul.

THE LANGUAGE OF SERVICE

How do people who are committed to service speak? They say:

- "I love you."
- "I forgive you."
- "Thank you."
- "Please, after you."
- "Please help me understand how I have offended you."
- "Let's work this out together."

THE ACTIVITIES OF SERVICE

Service is active. Acts of kindness speak with clarity and persuasiveness. Here are some actions to consider.

- Volunteer to go on a trek with the scouts.
- Share your expertise at a school or community center.
- Volunteer your services at a Hospice facility.
- Sing in the church choir.
- Volunteer for a short-term mission in a developing country.
- Teach a class.
- Coach a team.
- Become a consultant to a middle or high school business class.
- Take on a noble cause.
- Listen with CARE to others.
- Write a letter of kindness.

PUTTING SERVICE TO WORK

If you are serious about living a life of service, you can practice by applying the listening and conflict resolution models. Approach the person with whom you are having conflict. Share with that person that you would like to try a new way of working through your differences. Teach the conflict resolution model and then ask four questions: 1) Are you willing? 2) What do we want? 3) What if we did it this way or that way? 4) What do we do now to ensure success? Make sure you practice the CARE sequence of listening. See if the issue does not magically resolve and the relationship mature.

Epilogue

HEN WE FALL SHORT

THE PATH OF HUMILITY AND SPIRIT

We are all failures—at least, all the best of us are.

—J.M. Barrie

The window in our bathroom works only one way: we can see out, but the world can't see in. It's a practical arrangement; it offers us the dual benefit of privacy and a view of the pink-blossoming dogwood tree planted next to the window.

Every spring a little brown house sparrow visits the dogwood and looks at her reflection in the glass. When she can stand it no longer, she springs from her perch and throws herself into the windowpane. With legs akimbo she frantically flaps her wings to keep airborne. She manages to return to her perch to regain her senses and, yet, inconceivably, in the next moment dives into the image in the glass again.

Her more colorful male partner sits on a nearby branch and watches in disbelief as his beloved flies pell-mell into her own reflection.

As you begin living by the principles of personal discipline, there will likely be times when you are annoyed by your own flawed self-image. You may become disappointed in your progress; you may even be tempted to criticize yourself.

When you begin to doubt yourself, rather than engage in self-deprecation, look outward. Ask, "What can I do to help another?" That act of kindness will make your own image immensely more attractive—to you and to others.

FOUR PERSONAL LESSONS

I confess to being a bit of a perfectionist—okay, I'm an obsessive perfectionist: I like my nails trimmed, my shoes shinned, and my pants creased. I insist on high standards for any personal performance. When I go for a bicycle ride, I expect to set the pace. When I give a keynote presentation, I anticipate a standing ovation. I don't set out to be good, I set out to be dazzling, and when I fall short of my expectations, frequently I am miffed and bewildered.

Recently, when a friend of mine told me that he didn't like to "hang out" with me because he could never relax in my presence, I understood. I was a little hurt, but I understood. I can be intense. In my passion to live a life of discipline, I tend to alienate others.

My friend's disclosure reminded me, once again, to exercise caution when committing to a life of discipline: To make certain that my zeal for excellence does not interfere with my passion for people. As I strive to tap the power within—to be boldly disciplined—I am struck by the importance of two things: to practice humility and to serve from the spirit. When I fall short—when living a life of discipline becomes more ego- than spirit-driven—it is time to look outward, to redirect the flow of energy from self to others. Here are four lessons from my life:

1. Seek excellence without being didactic. Over the years, I have become so swept away by the potency of living a disciplined life that I am convinced that everyone should follow my lead, and occasionally I tell them so. But, thrusting my standards upon others doesn't make for enduring friendships. No one likes to be harangued—regardless of the nobility of the preachments.

Trusting that your audience will tell you when you cross the line is unreliable. Most people are exceedingly polite and will endure hours of diatribe before uttering a peep of resistance. (They will circumnavigate the globe to avoid crossing paths thereafter, but that is another matter.) Only a handful of my closest friends— those who have come to love me despite my missionary fervor— will eventually say, "Allen, give it a rest." No, it is up to the speaker to protect his audience from moralistic assaults.

The lesson for me, then, is to seek excellence for myself, yes, but to stop dicing my friends with my sacred saber of truth. Allow others the liberty to discover their own salvation, their own personal meaning, on their own terms.

2. Seek knowledge without being arrogant. I have a responsibility to learn continually. Whenever I am introduced to a great author, from classical to contemporary, I am astonished by my late arrival: How could I have missed this author? What has taken me so long? You mean, these ideas have been floating around all this time, and I'm just now learning about them? So when I make the acquaintance of a first-class mind and become virtual friends with the author, I am delighted.

Sometimes I am so captured by the new ideas that I wear them like a supercilious cloak of honor—as if to say, "That's right, I know what *supercilious* means (feeling or showing haughty disdain), and aren't you impressed."

Here's an arrogance-o-meter. The next time you are in conversation, work an obscure word into your patter: "Gee, you seem somewhat laconic today." Then observe your partner's response to what may be an unfamiliar word: look for fidgeting or widening of the eyes. Now, calibrate your own reaction. Are you pleased with yourself for having made your friend squirm? If the answer is "yes," even a provisional "yes," that's arrogance.

The lesson for me is to be humble as a learner, for although I may know what *supercilious* means, I haven't got a clue about *viral encephalitis* or *aseptic meningitis*, or a zillion other facts and figures within the walls of the Library of Congress (we are all illiterate about something). The trick is to be learned without being arrogant, for arrogance is just another word for ego. A humble learner does not seek to impress, but to validate the intelligence of the other.

3. Seek understanding without being judgmental. To genuinely understand another human being—to settle in comfortably and become familiar with his or her world—requires consummate humility. Too often we lumber into a series of pedantic judgments and, predictably, alienate others.

Judgments are multi-lingual. The most telling language—the language that shouts in our ears—is mute: the language of gestures and expressions: a grimace, a raised eyebrow, a glance.

My friend, George, tells me—in words and expressions—that he accepts me unconditionally, exactly as I am. I believe him, for in all the years that I have known him, he has never once tried to fix me—even when fixing was in order. I feel close to George—completely safe in his presence—because he has proven his commitment to unconditional love by consistently sidestepping judgment. The lesson is to be quiet in the sanctuary of another human being.

4. Seek to be vulnerable without being melodramatic. Asking a perfectionist to be vulnerable is like asking a great white shark to be gentle, more like, say, a koala bear. A perfectionist doesn't want to admit his shortcomings; if he did, he wouldn't be perfect anymore. But, then, perfection isn't the point, is it? Sure, we want to deal effectively with the challenges of our lives, but not without occasionally stubbing our toe in the middle of the night.

When you think about it, a life of perfection would be pretty drab. One of my favorite episodes from the popular, science fiction TV series, "The Twilight Zone," tells the tale of a gambler who dies and goes to what he (and the television viewers) believes to be heaven. He places his bet at the celestial crap table and, to his delight, rolls a seven. In fact, each and every time he places a wager, he wins. In the end, unrelenting winning become a diabolical nightmare.

"What kind of heaven is this?" he asks the house manager.

To which the demonic manager demurely responds, "What makes you think this is heaven?"

No, perfection is not the end in mind—that state would be hellishly boring; it is, rather, our ability to live with honor in challenging times.

Ironically, I always thought that my perfectionism would engender love; it does not—admiration, possibly, but never love. We love the people who, despite their character flaws or social awkwardness, manage to grow: the Rocky Balboa's, even the Archie Bunker's, of the world.

I have learned that to be loved, I must be vulnerable; I must be real, in the sense that a mountain or a stream or a sunrise is real: unpretentious, uncluttered, free of cultural propriety and political correctness—unable to be anything else but what they are. To be vulnerable is to be wholly transparent, willing to reveal aspirations and fears and even—in the most intimate of relationships—fantasies and transgressions.

Sublime transparency requires an escape from melodrama. Sometimes, we use vulnerability as an instrument of pity: if I can tell my story with enough histrionics—frenzy, rage, wretchedness—I will be rescued or, at least, coddled. That, of course, is not vulnerability, but, rather, manipulation. I am most vulnerable when I am least aware of my stage persona, when I am simply being me.

Now the power, and the real purpose, of being genuinely vulnerable is to grace others with the gift of one's self. The side benefit is the natural reciprocity that follows: vulnerability begets vulnerability, and mutual vulnerability begets love. (There is, of course, a caution: to select one's benefactors with care. Scoundrels can easily twist vulnerability into self-serving advantage. There is, however, a way to minimize the risk: If you are not sure that the other can be fully trusted, test the water first by sharing something relatively innocuous; if it is held sacred, take another tentative step into the deep end.)

So those are my sins: didacticism, arrogance, judgment, and occasionally melodrama. The list is pretty harrowing in the clear light of day, but not insurmountable. With an *attitude* of humility, a *goal* of benevolence, and the *disciplines* of love, responsibility, vision, commitment and service, I have the power within—the power that we all possess—to fulfill my mission as a "spiritual being having a human experience."

Bibliography

Block, Peter. *Stewardship: Choosing Service Over Self-Interest.* San Francisco: Berrett-Koehler Publishers, 1996.

Boorstin, Daniel J. *The Seekers: The Story of Man's Continuing Quest to Understand His World.* New York: Random House, 1998.

Buford, Bob. *Halftime: Changing Your Game Plan from Success to Significance.* Grand Rapids, Michigan: Zondervan Publishing House, 1994.

Collins, James C., and Jerry I. Porras. *Built to Last: Successful Habits of Visionary Companies.* New York: Harper Business, 1994.

Covey, Steven R. *The Seven Habits of Highly Effective People: Restoring the Character Ethic.* New York: Simon & Schuster, 1989.

Deutsch, M., and H. B. Gerard, "A Study of Normative and Informational Social Influences upon Individual Judgment." *Journal of Abnormal and Social Psychology,* 1955, 51, 629-636.

Dyer, Wayne. *Your Sacred Self: Making the Decision to Be Free.* New York: Harper Collins, 1995.

Freedman, J. L. "Long-term Behavioral Effects of Cognitive Dissonance." *Journal of Experimental Social Psychology*, 1966, 4, 195-203.

Glasser, William. *Control Theory: A New Explanation of How We Control Our Lives.* New York: Perennial Library, 1984.

Greenleaf, Robert K. *Servant Leadership: A Journey into the Nature of Legitimate Power and Greatness.* New York: Paulist Press, 1977.

Karpman, Stephen B. "Fairy Tales nd Script Drama Analysis," *Transactional Analysis Journal*, 1972, 2(2), 78-81.

McCarthy, Bernice. *The 4 MAT System: Teaching to Learning Styles with Right/Left Mode Techniques.* Excel, Inc., IL. 1987.

Milgram, Stanley. "Behavorial Study of Obedience." *Journal of Abnormal and Social Psychology*, 1963, 67, 371-378.

Peck, M. Scott. *The Different Drum: Community Making and Peace.* New York: Simon & Schuster, 1998.

Peck, M. Scott. *The Road Less Traveled: A New Psychology of Love, Traditional Values and Spiritual Growth.* New York: Simon & Schuster, 1978.

Rogers, Carl R. "A Theory of Therapy, Personality, and Interpersonal Relationships, as Developed in the Client-Centered Framework." In S. Koch (Ed.), *Psychology: A Study of a Science, Vol. III. Formulations of the Person and the Social Context.* New York: McGraw-Hill, 1959, 196.

About the Author

 Allen Johnson is founder and president of Johnson Dynamics, an organization and leadership development firm. He holds a master's in speech from the University of Washington and a Ph.D. in counseling psychology from Washington State University. A versatile professional, Allen specializes in the following:

- Keynote speaking on the topics of personal, interpersonal, and organizational effectiveness.
- Organizational consulting, featuring in-depth retreats on team and community building.
- Training on *The Power Within, The 25 Best Leadership and Management Tools in the Business, The Listening Course,* and *The Art of Speaking.*

Allen is also the author of *This Side of Crazy: Lessons on Living from Someone Who Should Know Better, But Keeps Messing Up Anyway.* He is an avid outdoorsman, passionate about mountain climbing, hiking, scuba diving, and bicycling. His favorite indoor activities—in addition to reading and writing—are playing the piano and singing.

Allen lives in Richland, Washington with his wife Nita.

Johnson Dynamics
2618 Quarterhorse Way
Richland, WA 99352
509-627-3000
Email: allenjohnsonphd@att.net
Website: http://members.theglobe.com/allenjohnson/go

Since 1984, *Executive Excellence* has provided business leaders and managers with the best and latest thinking on leadership development, managerial effectiveness, and organizational productivity. Each issue is filled with insights and answers from top business executives, trainers, and consultants—information you won't find in any other publication.

"Executive Excellence
is the *Harvard Business Review*
in *USA Today* format."

—Stephen R. Covey, author of *The 7 Habits of Highly Effective People*

"Executive Excellence
is the best executive advisory
newsletter anywhere in the world—
it's just a matter of time before a lot
more people find that out."

—Ken Blanchard, co-author
of *The One-Minute Manager*

**CONTRIBUTING
EDITORS INCLUDE**

Stephen R. Covey

Ken Blanchard

Peter Senge

Gifford Pinchot

Gary Hamel

Warren Bennis

INSTANT CONSULTANT

Now available on CD—15 years of powerful writings on leadership development, managerial effectiveness, and organ-izational productivity, written exclusively for today's leaders and managers. With the best and brightest business minds cross-referenced here, the Instant Consultant is a ready resource for dealing with day-to-day dilemmas $179.95

For more information please call Executive Excellence
Publishing at: **1-800-304-9782**
or visit our Web site: **www.eep.com**